GREAT
MYSTERIES

Robert Jackson

Quantum
Books

A QUANTUM BOOK

This book is produced by
Quantum Publishing Ltd.
6 Blundell Street
London N7 9BH

Copyright © MCMXCII
Quintet Publishing Limited.

This edition printed 2003

ISBN 1-86160-735-0

QUMGMG

Typeset in Britain by
Central Southern Typesetters, Eastbourne
Manufactured in Hong Kong by
Regent Publishing Services Ltd
Printed in China by
Leefung-Asco Printers Ltd

GREAT MYSTERIES

GHOSTS

Contents

Phantoms of the Ocean Storm

20th-century spectres – the USS *Forrestal*

S pectral ships, and vessels with ghostly stowaways, are firmly established among the legends of the sea. Most of these stories belong to the days of sailing ships, but one can find some more recent instances of supernatural happenings aboard ship.

A large, modern aircraft carrier, for example, is probably the last place you might expect to encounter a ghost, but there is said to be one lurking in a cargo hold on board the USS *Forrestal*, the first aircraft carrier built after World War II and also the first designed specifically to operate jet aircraft. Named after James V Forrestal, Secretary of the US Navy from 1944 to 1947, the carrier displaces 78,000 tons fully laden and is over 1,000 feet long. *Forrestal* carries a normal crew of 2,700, increased to 4,700 with the addition of a further 2,000 personnel assigned to her carrier air wing on operational duty.

Perhaps it isn't too surprising, then, that something the size of a small town should have a ghost. In the *Forrestal*'s case, the ghost is nicknamed George, allegedly after the former cargo division

● **BELOW** The mighty aircraft carrier USS *Forrestal* is said to be haunted. An unseen presence stalks the ship's No 1 and No 3 holds, moving objects and switching lights on and off. The haunting may be connected with an incident that occurred in 1967, when 134 sailors lost their lives in an explosion.

● RIGHT The spectral *Flying Dutchman* has been sighted many times over the years, turning up all over the world. The phantom has been seen in Galveston Bay, Texas, where she was sighted twice in 1892.

officer, Lieutenant George Conway – who, incidentally, is still very much alive. The haunted areas are the carrier's holds, No 1 and No 3, which are found deep below the waterline. Although no spectral figure has been seen, strange things happen down below; lights go on and off unexpectedly, doors open and shut for no apparent reason, and several crew members over the years have openly admitted to being terrified of "something" while on duty down there. One man, climbing a ladder leading to an upper deck, felt his leg seized by something unseen; it took considerable effort before he could free himself. Another felt an invisible hand tap him on the shoulder.

The *Forrestal* haunting could be connected with a serious accident that occurred on board the carrier on the morning of 25 July, 1967, when the ship was on operational duty off Vietnam. Aircraft were being made ready for a sortie when a rocket from an F-4 Phantom jet was accidentally fired into the fuel tank of an A-4 Skyhawk, which exploded. The whole after-end of the ship was soon engulfed in fire as the wind carried the flames to other jets, which then exploded in turn. Many men were blown overboard by the explosion or trapped in compartments below and burned to death.

Destroyer escorts closed in to spray water over the burning carrier while flight-deck personnel worked with great gallantry amid exploding bombs and acres of burning petrol to bring the main flight-deck fire under control in less than an hour, but it was a further twelve hours before secondary fires below were extinguished. One hundred and thirty-four men were killed on the *Forrestal* that day. Perhaps the ghost that wanders the mighty ship is the lost soul of one of them.

Can a ship itself have a soul – and is it possible that it might be condemned to wander the oceans for ever? This certainly seems true of one famous phantom.

July 11, 1881. During the middle watch the **Flying Dutchman** *crossed our bows. She first appeared as a strange, red light, as of a ship all aglow, in the midst of which light the masts, spars and sails, seemingly those of a normal brig, some two hundred yards distant from us, stood out in strong relief as she came up. The look-out man on the forecastle reported her as close on the port bow, where also the officer of the watch from the bridge clearly saw her, as did also the quarter-deck midshipman, who was sent forward at once to the forecastle to report back. But on arriving there, no vestige nor any sign of any material ship was to be seen. The early morning, as the night had been, was clear, the sea strangely calm.*

So reads the log of the Royal Navy warship HMS *Bacchante*, cruising in the Pacific, one of many vessels which have encountered the most celebrated sea-borne spectre.

According to legend, the *Flying Dutchman* – the name refers both to the ghost ship and its captain – has its origin in one of two real-life characters. The first was a Dutch sea captain called Vanderdecken, a contemporary of the 17th-century Admiral Tromp, who was condemned to sail the oceans forever because he was godless and a notorious blasphemer; the second was a mariner named Bernard Fokke, who allegedly made a pact with the devil so that he could reach the East Indies in 90 days.

The *Flying Dutchman* has cropped up all over the world, including Galveston Bay, Texas, where she was seen twice in 1892. Sometimes, the captain himself has been seen on her poop, glowing with a ghastly light, his face twisted with malevolence as he lets forth screams of maniacal laughter.

● LEFT A 19th-century engraving depicting the *Flying Dutchman*. The name refers both to the ship and its captain, and may have its origin in one of two real-life characters. One of them was Bernard Fokke, who was supposed to have made a pact with the devil in order to reach the East Indies in 90 days.

Ghostly derelicts

On the night of 27 September, 1860, the American whaler *George Henry* was at anchor in Frobisher Bay, on the southern tip of Baffin Island, riding out a severe storm. She had set sail from Hudson Bay and headed northwards for Arctic waters with the intention of searching for the ill-fated expedition led by the British navigator Sir John Franklin, which had disappeared mysteriously on its way to the North Pole. With the *George Henry* was a supply ship, the *Rescue*, which had the reputation of being an unlucky ship; most of her voyages had ended in death for at least one of her crew members.

As the storm worsened, the skipper of the *George Henry*, Captain Hall, decided to take the *Rescue*'s crew on board. It was just as well that he did. A short while later, the *Rescue* dragged her anchor and began to drift slowly towards the rocky, wave-lashed shore. For hours, as though possessed by some strange intelligence, she fought the onslaught of the wind and sea. Then, with awful finality, a huge wave caught her and hurled her against the rocks. Gradually, as the waves pounded over her and ripped away her masts, the driving snow spread over her like a shroud.

grimly familiar outline, with its broken masts sticking up like pointed, accusing fingers. It was the *Rescue*.

She was following an arrow-straight course, as though she was being steered by some steady hand. But there was no sign of anyone on deck, and the only sure way to find out whether the hulk was manned or not would be for someone to go aboard her. The very idea sent shivers up and down the sailors' spines, and there were no volunteers. In silence, the men watched the spectral ship as it was swallowed up once more in the chill mist.

That same evening, the *George Henry* dropped anchor in Frobisher Bay, not far from the spot where the unlucky *Rescue* had been dashed against the rocks the previous year. A few hours later, a severe gale blew up from the north-north-east, driving great blocks of ice across the sea in front of it. Desperately, the sailors rushed to the side and tried to fend off the biggest of the blocks.

And then they saw the *Rescue*. She came sliding out of the gloom about a mile away, her ghostly appearance enhanced by the wan moonlight that shone on her. To the terrified sailors, it seemed that she was herding the ice-blocks before her. And, what was worse, she was heading straight for the *George Henry*.

Helplessly, the seamen could only watch as the menacing shape of the derelict came relentlessly towards them. They seemed spellbound by the approach of what, to them, seemed a kind of supernatural premonition of doom. They could hear the creaking and groaning of the *Rescue*'s timbers now, and the angry sound seemed like the vengeful voice of the battered hulk itself. Within minutes, the men expected that they would be struggling for their survival in the icy water when the two vessels collided.

Then the miracle happened. Abruptly, just as the two ships were on the point of touching, the *Rescue* veered away. Scraping past the whaler by a hair's breadth, she disappeared into the shadows. Perhaps she had struck a block of ice, and been thrown off course. But to the sailors, it seemed as though some ghostly helmsman had relented at the last moment.

The next day, Captain Hall weighed anchor and sailed out of the bay. There was no sign of the *Rescue*; perhaps she had gone to the bottom at last. But the encounters with the derelict had had an

● **ABOVE** A phantom vessel appears on the horizon. Sometimes, such "phantoms" turned out to be real ships, abandoned by their crews to drift aimlessly on the ocean currents before succumbing to the effects of wind and weather.

The next morning, she was nowhere to be seen. Perhaps, covered by layers of snow, her outline blended with the rocky background. But the sailors were convinced that she had been pounded to bits, and the *George Henry* sailed on alone.

Ten months later, in July 1861, the *George Henry* was once again in the area of Baffin Island. Suddenly, the look-out gave a wild cry of alarm, pointing at a black, sinister shape that loomed up out of the long shadows less than two miles away. Even at this distance, there was no mistaking that uncanny effect on the sailors. They were silent and morose, their eyes turning fearfully towards the horizon time and again.

Then, as dusk was falling, they saw the dreaded hulk once more, quite close to the spot where she had been abandoned months before. The following morning, she was seen to be drifting out towards the open sea. An hour later, the seamen lost sight of her for good.

No one knows what happened to the *Rescue* in the end. Some old seafarers claim that her grim spectre still haunts the seas around Baffin Island. The influence that derelicts exert on the lore of the sea is so strong that even today, well over a hundred years later, many a young sailor who is on watch during the long night hours in that freezing ocean waste just below the Arctic Circle, and who knows the old story, half expects to see that menacing black form drifting towards him out of the frosty mist.

Many other derelicts, drifting around the sea-lanes for years, gave rise to tales of phantom ships. Sightings declined sharply in the 1930s, when the US Coast Guard embarked on a programme to track down and sink such abandoned vessels in North American waters, so removing hazards to shipping. But there are others which cannot be hunted down, nor explained away; vessels like the *Young Teazer*, an American privateer. In 1813,

trapped by warships of the Royal Navy in Mahone Bay, she was destroyed by her skipper, Lieutenant Johnson, who blew up her magazine and himself with it. Since then, the phantom of the *Young Teazer* has often been sighted off Nova Scotia, approaching ships at sea and then veering away in flames.

● **RIGHT** A frightened helmsman sees a ghost ship coming up over the horizon. In the 1930s, sightings of "phantom" ships declined dramatically when the US Coast Guard embarked on a programme to track down and destroy derelict vessels.

Phantom sailors

Phantom sailors are much more rare than phantom ships, but when they manifest themselves it is usually in dramatic – and helpful – form, as though they still belong to the brotherhood of the sea. One such saved the life of Captain Joshua Slocum.

On 2 July, 1895, Slocum set course south-eastwards into the Atlantic from Yarmouth, Nova Scotia, on the first leg of what was to be a voyage around the world. His craft, a 36-foot sloop named *Spray*, had lain rotting in a field for seven years before he had lovingly restored her.

It was pride that had driven Slocum to make his single-handed attempt to circle the globe; pride in the days when he used to skim across the oceans ahead of the trade winds in the white-winged clippers that had been life and breath to him. Then

the new age had dawned – the age of steam. And suddenly, Joshua Slocum had found himself out of a job. He had not been able to adapt to the new era. He couldn't bear to think of the majestic sailing ships being swept from the world's oceans by smoke-belching iron monsters. There had been no prospect of another seagoing command for Slocum. The *Spray*, and his lone voyage round the world, combined in his last adventure.

For two days out of Yarmouth everything went well – and then the storm broke. It blew up without warning, screaming down across the surface of the sea from the barren wastes of the north-east and driving towering waves before it. The heaving, surging water seized the little sloop and spun her like a cork.

For three days Slocum battled his way through it in a black haze of fatigue, losing all count of time. At last, reeling with exhaustion, he tumbled into his bunk and waited for the death that now seemed inevitable.

A long time later, he opened his eyes. Outside, the storm still howled and great waves still slammed into the *Spray* – but the sloop seemed to be riding smoothly through the heaving sea. Puzzled, Slocum dragged himself across the cabin and peered up into the cockpit. Cold fear gripped him.

Standing with legs firmly planted on the heaving deck, both hands grasping the wheel, was a man.

In the dusk, Slocum saw that he was tall and heavily built – and that he was wearing the type of clothing that belonged to the 15th or 16th century.

For several minutes, Slocum could only stand and stare at the shadowy figure. At last, summoning all his courage, he demanded to know who the stranger was. It was some time before the apparition answered. When it did, its voice seemed to come from a great distance away. "I am the helmsman of the *Pinta*," it said.

Later, Slocum could not remember with any certainty whether the stranger had actually spoken, or whether the ghostly voice had sounded in his own mind. He racked his brains, trying to remember where he had heard the name *Pinta* before. Then suddenly, with a shock, it came to him. The *Pinta* had been one of the three ships under the command of Christopher Columbus when he set out to find the New World in 1492.

Slowly, steadying his whirling senses, Joshua Slocum raised his eyes to look at the phantom helmsman, but the shadowy figure had vanished. Then, strangely, Slocum felt new strength flowing back into his body. Stepping forward, he grasped the wheel once more, guiding the little sloop through the turbulent seas, confident now that he was going to survive. Just a few hours later, the storm died away.

Fifty-one-year-old Slocum, who incidentally was a non-swimmer, went on to complete his perilous voyage round the world – the first lone sailor to do so. He landed at Newport, Rhode Island, on 3 July 1898 after covering a total distance of 46,000 miles.

A few years later, he set out in the *Spray* once again, to sail from Rhode Island to the West Indies. It should have been an easy trip; the weather along his route was exceptionally calm. But Slocum never reached his destination. Perhaps, once again, he met the ghostly helmsman of the *Pinta* – and perhaps this time he had been steered not to safety, but to disaster.

Just 33 years after Slocum's encounter with the ghostly stowaway, in 1928, another solitary voyager had an equally strange experience. He was a German named Franz Romer, and he had set out from Portugal in a simple kayak fitted with a sail, bound for America. Off the Canary Islands, Romer suddenly found himself fighting for his life in the raging heart of a storm. Worn out by lack of sleep, uncertain of his position, he went on steering the frail craft like an automaton – aware that if it capsized, he would not have the strength to right it again.

● BELOW Captain Joshua Slocum, who claimed that his life was saved in mid-ocean by the spectral appearance of the helmsman of the *Pinta*, one of the ships that set out with Christopher Columbus to discover the Americas.

● LEFT Slocum's 36-foot sloop, the *Spray*. The craft had lain rotting in a field for seven years before Slocum lovingly restored her to take on his record-breaking voyage around the world. The *Spray*, and Slocum, were lost at sea several years later.

And then, in the middle of the howling night, he heard the voice. Rousing himself from his stupor, he peered around him in the darkness, expecting to see a ship – but there was nothing. The voice came again, a quiet, coaxing voice, urging him to alter course and steer due south instead of south-east.

On an impulse, Romer obeyed – and at dawn, when the storm died down, he sighted Palma, the most westerly of the Canaries. Looking at his chart, he saw with a shock that if he had continued on his original course, the storm would have dashed him to pieces on the jagged rocks of a small island.

Were the phantom helmsman and the voice from the night that saved the lives of Slocum and Romer really spirits from beyond – or were they hallucinations, products of a mind tired almost beyond endurance, flashing a warning of impending disaster from the deep recesses of the subconscious to the physical senses? We shall never know. But strange things, including miracles, can happen to a man alone on the immensity of the ocean.

To be confronted by a ghost – that is to say a visible spectre – is alarming enough, but to be the target of unseen forces can be far more frightening. Such occurrences come under the general heading of poltergeist activity, which is almost always associated with the uncontrolled and subliminal release of psychic energy from a distressed human being.

The name poltergeists means literally "noisy spirits", and they are a world-wide phenomenon. Their activity generally follows a definite pattern; furniture and household objects are displaced, crockery is smashed, taps are turned on and off mysteriously, strange noises are heard. Sometimes, the poltergeist writes messages.

● BELOW This French illustration shows poltergeist activity in the form of cutlery flying around a child asleep in its cradle. Such activity may sometimes be generated by the subconscious mind, releasing forces over which it has no control.

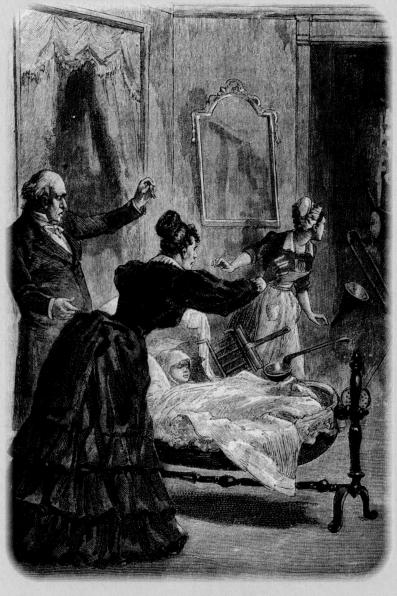

Polter-geist!

Malevolent spirits – the *Tokolosi*

There is nothing humorous about one type of poltergeist that features prominently in African folklore. Known as the *Tokolosi*, it is a spirit of unbelievable malevolence, with the power to drive people insane. There are many well-documented tales about it; one of them concerned a little girl called Mary, who lived with her parents on a farm near George, in South Africa's Cape Province. The family were natives of Hottentot descent.

The trouble began one evening when the family sat down to a meal. Mary was just reaching out to take a potato from a bowl when suddenly a large clod of earth appeared from nowhere and thudded down on the table beside her. The little girl gave a cry of fright. Puzzled and alarmed, her father, Andrew, looked up at the ceiling; there was nothing to indicate where the lump of earth might have come from. But Andrew was not a man to worry about things he was unable to explain; he simply brushed the clod of earth aside and went on with the meal.

But there was more trouble in store for his daughter. As she raised her cup to her lips, some unseen force dashed it out of her hand and smashed it on the earthen floor. The little girl jumped to her feet in alarm – and as she did so, something knocked her chair flying across the room and sent her staggering with a vicious shove.

The same thing happened the next day, and the day after. The little girl began to look physically ill; more than that, she was in a state of constant terror. She would wake up in the night, screaming in fear. In desperation, seeing the girl grow more poorly every day and in apparent danger of being driven out of her mind, Andrew turned for help to

his boss, a forthright man named Major Williams who was not noted for his belief in spirits of any kind. Although he was convinced that Mary was the victim of some natural mental disorder rather than a supernatural influence, Williams agreed to visit Andrew's home. The man was obviously badly disturbed about something, and Williams thought that he might be able to sort out the trouble in some way.

Williams told Andrew that he wanted to be alone with the girl for a while, and sent the man and his wife off on an errand. Mary was in bed; Williams bolted the door of the hut, sat down on a chair and began to talk quietly to the girl. After a while, he noticed that she was no longer listening to him. Her eyes, glazed in sheer terror, were fixed on a corner of the room. Williams turned around, but there was nothing to be seen. And then a sensation

● **FAR RIGHT** For a long time, scientists and paranormal researchers have tried to establish the cause of spontaneous combustion, when objects and sometimes people are consumed by fire for no apparent reason. This photograph shows damage caused by spontaneous combustion in Brazil.

● **RIGHT** A "phantom stone-throwing" incident in Paris. Although this phenomenon is often associated with poltergeist activity, it may be caused by other underlying forces – perhaps emanating from strong fluctuations in the earth's magnetic field.

of pure horror ran through him as some invisible thing which he later described as "furry and infinitely loathsome" brushed past his face.

The next instant, Mary let out a piercing scream. There was an audible thud and she fell back on the bed, clutching her chest. Williams flung open the door and sunlight came pouring into the hut to reveal an ugly red mark on the little girl's skin.

Somehow, Williams managed to calm the terrified girl. By the time Andrew and his wife returned, she was in an exhausted sleep. Williams told Mary's parents that she would be better off in hospital, and that he would arrange to take her there the following day. But when he came to the hut the next day, Andrew and his family had vanished.

Weeks passed, and still they did not return. It began to look as though the *Tokolosi* had driven them away for good.

Then, one day about three months later, Williams saw a familiar figure coming through the farm gate. It was Andrew, and he was smiling again. Jubilantly, he told Williams that the evil spirit had been exorcised by a powerful witch doctor. Moreover, the witch doctor had discovered that the *Tokolosi* had been the product of the hatred of Andrew's mother-in-law, who had wanted the little girl to live with her as an unpaid slave. The mother-in-law had been threatened with all manner of horrible fates by the witch doctor, and had been soundly thrashed by Andrew into the bargain, and all was well again.

Friendly pranks

Usually, poltergeists are far more benevolent than the dreaded *Tokolosi*. The poltergeist phenomenon crops up frequently in English inns: one haunts the Holman Clavel Inn, near the village of Blagdon, Somerset. One of its manifestations is described in Marc Alexander's book *Haunted Inns*; the words are those of the landlord, John Clapp.

"There was an American writer and his wife staying here. When they decided to go back to the States they had a lot of stuff to take back with them and they asked us to get rid of a load of books which they no longer had any use for.

Being quite expensive books, I did not want to throw them away. One of them was on forestry and, as one of the regulars here is a timber-feller with his own business, I asked him if he would like the book. He said he would, but as he was riding a motor cycle that evening he would pick it up the next day when he had his car. So I put the book under the counter, and the following evening when he came in there was no book to be found, although we looked everywhere for it.

At first I thought someone must have moved it so I said I'd find that book if it took all day. I thought I might have put it back with the other books in the cellar and forgotten about it, so I checked them. No sign of it. I checked the wine cellar and gradually made my way through the

whole pub. I was so determined to find it that I went on searching for about a month.

Number 5 bedroom upstairs had a television set in it so my wife could watch it and do her ironing at the same time. One night she turned round and there was the missing book, on top of the wardrobe. I would certainly never have put it there, and neither would she. And who would have wanted to take a book from under the bar, hide it and then weeks later sneak into the bedroom and put it on the wardrobe? Things disappear and then turn up months and months later. Once the key of a box disappeared. It was missing for two or three years and then one morning there it was, right in the middle of the carpet on the floor of the bar."

● **LEFT** Poltergeist activity at Dodleston, Chester, May 1985, where all manner of objects were moved about or overturned.

● RIGHT Damage caused by poltergeist activity in May 1985. Not all poltergeists cause malicious damage; often, objects are moved by mysterious forces and then returned unharmed to their original places, days and sometimes weeks later.

The pranks at the Holman Clavel (the name derives from two Old English words, *helme* meaning holly and *clavel* meaning a recess) are attributed to the spirit of a defrocked monk, affectionately known as Charlie. He is said to get up to all sorts of tricks, including playing a solitary game of bowls at dead of night in the alley adjoining the inn.

In 1894, a poltergeist with a sense of humour plagued the tenants of a cottage at Durweston, in Dorset, England. One day, a gamekeeper called Newman was in the cottage when a boot came flying in through the door. The tenant threw it out and Newman put his foot on it, defying anything to move it. As soon as he took his foot away the boot flew up and knocked his hat off. The same game-keeper witnessed another phenomenon at the cottage – objects propelling themselves through the air incredibly slowly.

"I saw coming from behind the door a quantity of little shells. They came round the door from a height of about five feet. They came one at a time. They came very slowly, and when they hit me I could hardly feel them. They came so slowly, that in the ordinary way they would have dropped long before they reached me."

Amityville – fact or fiction?

But can a house itself generate poltergeist activity on a frightening scale? It certainly seemed to be the case with a colonial-style house in Amityville, Long Island, New York, which was the scene of a terrible multiple murder in 1974. On 13 November that year, 23-year-old Ronald DeFeo, Jr, cold-bloodedly killed his father, mother, two sisters and two brothers as they lay in their beds. He was subsequently sentenced to 150 years in prison.

● ABOVE The "haunted house" at Amityville. The whole episode was later found to be an elaborate hoax, a publicity stunt on a large scale. Oddly enough, some of the principal characters later died mysterious or tragic deaths.

A few weeks after the trial, the house on South Shore was purchased by George and Kathleen Lutz, who moved in with their three children at the time around Christmas. Just 28 days later they moved out – driven out, they claimed, by evil forces. From the very first night, they said, they had been disturbed by strange and terrifying phenomena. It began with peculiar noises, soon to be followed by the inexplicable opening and closing of doors and windows. Evil red eyes peered at them through their windows from the darkness beyond, and in the snow outside they found the prints of cloven hooves. Hideous green slime oozed from the ceiling, and through keyholes.

The case – which quickly became known as the Amityville Horror in the press – later achieved worldwide notoriety in a book and film. The Parapsychology Institute of America (PIA) became involved at George Lutz's request, agreeing to investigate the haunting of the house by what Lutz described as "demons", but a few days later Lutz cancelled the investigation on the grounds that he did not want any publicity.

But publicity there was, and plenty of it. The media turned the house in Amityville into a kind of national horror shrine, and the public loved it. A lot of people made a lot of money, both from the original tale and sequels based on it. Dr Stephen Kaplan, who in 1976 was the executive director of the PIA, carried out a personal investigation into the affair, and concluded that the horror story was pure invention. But by this time there were too many people on the money-spinning Amityville bandwagon; its momentum went on increasing.

The next occupants of the "house of horror", Jim and Barbara Cromarty, made a huge joke of the whole affair, even though sightseers had at first made their life intolerable. In fact, they brought a legal action against the former owners, and eventually their claim was settled out of court. The Cromartys took great delight in holding Hallowe'en parties at the house, showing guests the places where the alleged poltergeist and "demonic" activity was supposed to have occurred.

And yet, in the wake of all the publicity and money-making, some strange things befell those who had been involved in the original horror story. Jay Anson, author of *The Amityville Horror* best-seller, died soon after receiving a million-dollar advance for his next book. Paul Hoffman, who wrote the original feature article, died some time later in mysterious circumstances. The Cromartys' son, David, who had lived in Ronald DeFeo Jr's bedroom, died tragically early. Perhaps evil forces were at work in Amityville, after all.

● RIGHT The Mulhouse poltergeist case, France. A sheet of paper with drawings on was found folded inside a sealed camera, from which the film had disappeared.

Destruction and damage

In Wales at Coedkernew, Gwent, a farmhouse was afflicted by a troublesome poltergeist in 1904. Bundles of hay were thrown into the yard, pictures were turned around on the walls, 200 pieces of crockery were dropped in the kitchen without being broken, beds were moved and some carried out on to the landing, baking soda was put in a tub of lard, pickled cabbage was mixed with cream, and the name of the woman's first husband was traced on the sooty glass of a lamp. One night, ten

● BELOW Poltergeist activity at Dodleston, Chester, May 1985, when computer messages were received from a man living in the 16th century.

people – including the village policeman – sat up to keep vigil in the farmhouse. Several hours passed with nothing extraordinary happening – then a pat of butter flew across the room and hit the policeman in the eye.

For 18 months, beginning late in 1979, a very destructive poltergeist drove a woman named Mrs Adams, in her 80s, and her 50-year-old daughter Pauline to the verge of distraction at their home in Reading, about 40 miles (65 km) from London. First of all, the poltergeist began to move furniture; then it began to smash things. It smashed TV sets and radios and destroyed crockery and glassware, often bombarding the two women as they sat downstairs, yet without causing any injury. It broke furniture; it switched off the electricity and then turned it on again; it caused clocks to stop and the bathroom to flood; it engineered a gas leak that could not be traced and cured it just as mysteriously; it tore money (including Pauline's holiday money) to shreds or made it disappear; and it stole clothes.

The two women were not the only ones to experience the poltergeist activity. One day, Mrs Adams's 17-year-old grandson, Stephen, was standing in the living room when every shred of clothing except his underpants flew off his body and vanished. Instinctively, he cried out, "Give me back my clothes!" or words to that effect – and the items

suddenly reappeared one by one, draping themselves over the top of the door. Thirteen shoes also reappeared – all but one of seven pairs that had belonged to Pauline. They had mysteriously vanished over the previous months.

As time went by, the attacks on people grew more vicious. Mrs Adams received a cut on the head from a flying tablet box; a family friend was struck in the face by a packet of butter that shot out of her shopping basket. Priests and mediums were called in to try and exorcise the poltergeist, but its activity continues almost unabated. Finally, in desperation, the two ladies moved house, and the poltergeist ceased to torment them.

Not all "well-documented" cases of poltergeist activity turn out to be genuine. One of the more controversial cases centred on Borley Rectory in Essex, which at one time had the reputation of being the most haunted house in England. Built in 1862 on what some believe to have been the site of an old monastery, it had a long history of hauntings until it was destroyed by fire in 1939, and the ruins were finally demolished in 1944. The hauntings, particularly in the form of poltergeist activity, reached a crescendo after 1929, when a veteran ghost-hunter named Harry Price took over the tenancy. Charles Sutton, then a reporter on the *Daily Mail*, provided a plausible explanation.

● BELOW Spontaneous combustion that occurred in a house in Cheshire, England, in 1952 was thought to be the result of poltergeist activity. Disturbances continued even when the police set traps and kept watch. The poltergeist was fond of moving furniture around.

● RIGHT Borley Rectory, which was reputed to be the most haunted house in England. Built in 1862, it had a long history of hauntings until it was destroyed by fire in 1939. Some of the later hauntings were hoaxes perpetrated by the rectory's owner, Harry Price, but the earlier ones remain unexplained.

● BELOW Borley Rectory pictured after the fire that destroyed it. The ruins were finally demolished in 1944. The original building was said to have been built on the site of an ancient monastery.

"From Harry Price, self-styled Director of the National Laboratory of Psychical Research, I learned that in a haunted house you need have no fear of the ghost but you must beware of the ghost's earthly publicity agents. Many things happened in the night I spent in the famous Borley Rectory with Harry Price and one of his colleagues, including one uncomfortable moment when a large pebble hit me on the head.

After much noisy 'phenomena' I seized Harry and found his pockets full of bricks and pebbles. This was one 'phenomenon' he could not explain, so I rushed to the nearest village to 'phone the Daily Mail with my story, but after a conference with the lawyer my story was killed. The News Editor said: 'Bad luck, old man, but there were two of them and only one of you.'"

For every poltergeist hoax, however, there are a dozen cases that appear to be genuine. Doubtless, some can be explained away by natural causes; for example, houses – particularly old houses – produce mysterious tapping and groaning noises within their structural framework. Creatures such as rodents and birds, move around in their secret places.

But they do not make crockery fly through the air, nor do they move heavy furniture from one room to another. What we call the poltergeist phenomenon is a fact, and it merits deep investigation. Somehow – no one yet knows how or why – it is triggered by a powerful human psyche. On one occasion, it administered a profound shock to an entire nation.

It happened in 1976, when a young psychic named Matthew Manning went on Japanese television to demonstrate his extraordinary energy-channelling talents. A few minutes into the 90-minute programme, which had been delayed for some time because the camera trolley kept blowing its fuse, a panic-stricken viewer phoned the TV

● THIS PAGE A famous incident involving poltergeist activity at Mulhouse, France, produced a number of interesting phenomena from 1955 to 1981. The activities centred around a girl named Carla. She is seen here (below) with an automatic drawing of her son; this creative work later replaced uncontrolled poltergeist activity. A safety pin and lock of hair belonging to no-one in the family, was found in the cellar, while graffiti appeared on the floor while Carla was in a hypnotic trace (above.)

● **BELOW** Matthew Manning, the psychic who released poltergeist activity all over Japan in the course of a 90-minute TV programme. It may be that he unlocked hidden forces in the minds of millions of viewers, unleashing a "psychic storm".

● **ABOVE** Another incident from the Mulhouse, France. Eight inches of soil had to be dug out before the cellar door could be opened, after the ground level had inexplicably risen.

station to say that the ashtray in front of her TV set had suddenly split in two with a loud bang. After that, calls flooded in with details of similar phenomena, many of which were later investigated. A company executive and seven witnesses told how a cigarette packet on the table before them had divided in half, as though cut by a knife. Elsewhere, money burst into flames spontaneously, bottles crashed to the floor from shelves, light bulbs burst, taps turned themselves on and off, car engines started with no ignition key in them. In other cases, objects disappeared or materialized. In one instance, rice jumped out of a bowl and hung poised in mid-air before the astonished eyes of the would-be diner.

The phenomena lasted for the full 90 minutes of Manning's programme, then abruptly ceased. The unanswered question remains: did Manning's psyche alone cause the nationwide outburst of poltergeist activity – or did he unlock hidden forces in the minds of millions of people throughout Japan, unleashing a kind of psychic storm that made the impossible happen?

Phantom Missiles and Phantom Sounds

Instances of "phantom" stone-throwing are by no means rare; neither are they a modern phenomenon. One recorded case dates from 1682, when George Walton, an inhabitant of Portsmouth, New Hampshire, was subjected to such a deluge. One Sunday night in June, a fierce and unexpected shower of stones rattled against the sides and roof of the Walton household. Walton and his family dashed outside, but found nothing. As they stood there in bright moonlight, another shower of stones hurtled around their heads. They rushed back inside and barred the doors and windows, waiting fearfully for what would happen next.

Suddenly, more stones came crashing through the windows and down the chimney, rebounding around the room. The bombardment continued at intervals, for about four hours. Overcoming their fear, Walton and the other members of his family collected the stones and placed them in a pile; they were found to be very hot to the touch.

At about two o'clock in the morning, Walton, noticing that the bombardment seemed to be confined to his living-room, decided that the best thing to do was to retire to bed and wait for daylight. He had just turned in when a heavy stone came hurtling through his bedroom door. He got out of bed to pick it up, but it suddenly levitated and shot into a neighbouring room. According to a guest who was

● **BELOW** Investiging a stone-throwing incident at Carapicuiba, Brazil, in September 1974. The "stone-throwing" phenomenon is worldwide, with well-documented cases originating in the Americas, Europe, Africa and Australasia.

the principal eye-witness outside Walton's family, and who later wrote an account of the happenings, the attacks persisted for several days. The main target seemed to be Walton himself; he occasionally had to dodge volleys of flying stones while working in the fields away from the house. In keeping with the superstition of the times, the whole affair was blamed on witchcraft, Walton having earned the enmity of an old woman by taking a strip of land from her.

One person on the receiving end of a savage bombardment was Gilbert Smith, an aboriginal, who lived with his wife and seven children in a three-roomed wooden cottage on the farm where he worked, some 200 miles (320 km) from Perth in Australia's Upper Blackwood district. Smith was an excellent shearer, and an intelligent and thoroughly trustworthy man.

It was in the evening of 17 May, 1955, that the stone-throwing began – and plunged the Smith family into a mystery that has never been solved. That evening, Smith's wife, Jean, was gathering wood near the cottage when she was startled by a sudden thud. Thinking that someone had thrown something at her, she ran back into the house – and, as she went inside, she heard a sharp crack as though a stone had struck the wall.

It was dark outside, and her husband went out to look around. He walked all around the house, but there was nothing to be seen or heard. Perplexed, he went back indoors – and was to get the shock of his life. In one corner of the room lay an old golf ball, one of his children's playthings. Suddenly, for no reason at all, it flew across the room and struck the opposite wall with a resounding crack. A second later, there was a loud thud as though something heavy had landed on the roof.

Smith was even more puzzled and frightened by the fact that his two dogs were making no noise at all. If there had been anyone outside, the animals would have been raising a fearful racket. Telling his wife to stay indoors, Smith jumped into his battered old van and set off into the night, intent on bringing back some neighbours as reinforcements. He had only been gone a few minutes when one of the dogs began to bark and howl, thrashing around wildly at the end of its chain. Plucking up all her courage, Jean went outside and turned the animal loose. With a last howl, it disappeared into the darkness like a rocket.

Jean went back inside – seconds later the mysterious thuds began again. Seizing her husband's rifle, she cautiously peered around the door – an empty jam jar flew past, missing her head by inches, shattering into fragments against the wall. Terrified, Jean ducked quickly back indoors and bolted the door as more uncanny thuds shook the house.

● BELOW Stone axes found at a prehistoric site in Brittany. Flying stones and mysterious noises are often associated with such sites.

● **LEFT** Strange prehistoric circles, looking like ghostly eyes when seen from the air, were carved into the Wiltshire chalk by a long-dead race. Wiltshire is one of the world's leading centres of paranormal activity.

Gilbert came back some time later, bringing his neighbour and the latter's whole family with him. They barricaded themselves in the house and waited for the noises to stop – but they went on all night, making it impossible for anyone to get any sleep. When daylight came, there was a lull in the mysterious attacks. The men ventured outside and carried out a thorough search around the house, but they found nothing.

The unearthly bombardment began again the following evening, soon after dark. This time, Smith's boss was present. At first, he had laughed when he heard the shearer's story, but he wasn't laughing any more. This time, the stones actually appeared inside the house. They did not fly in through the door or windows – they just appeared suddenly in mid-air and fell to the floor.

The bombardment went on night after night, and now the mysterious attacks began to affect the house of Smith's neighbour, Alf Krakour. The stones were quite small compared to those that struck Smith's home, but they were red-hot to the touch. And the most frightening thing of all was that they began to come in through the walls – without leaving any holes.

Inevitably, the newspapers got hold of the story. For several days the area swarmed with reporters, but for some reason none came at night, when the weird activity was at its peak. There was absolutely nothing for them to see or hear during the daytime, and after a while they lost interest.

Among the visitors to the Smith and Krakour households were six members of the Perth Psychic Research Society, who declared that the activity was similar to poltergeist activity reported from other parts of the world. This knowledge did nothing to comfort the Smiths and Krakours; all they knew was that the stone-throwing showed no sign of ceasing and that the stone seemed to be getting bigger. On one occasion, a 40-pound rock drifted down like a feather onto Smith's roof without making even the smallest dent.

Apart from that, the affair now took a new turn. Mysterious lights were seen, hovering in the distance or racing across the night sky. When the lights were in the vicinity, the air seemed to vibrate with strange, barely audible whistling noises. And all the while, the stones went on falling – sometimes as many as 150 in a single night.

The frightening bombardment went on for over a year. Then, abruptly, the stone-throwing ceased. But for the Smiths and the Krakours, their nerves shattered, life would never be the same again.

Mysterious bombardments by stones have been associated with poltergeist activity; in fact, they are quite different manifestations of supernatural forces. In moving or throwing objects, a poltergeist appears to have a malevolent, or at best mischievous, purpose; its target is often an individual person. Showers of stones, on the other hand, although they may appear to target a specific house or area, occur more or less at random.

The Ontario Witch Balls

A century and a half after George Walton and his family were plagued by the mysterious hail of stones, a similar phenomenon beset farmer John McDonald in the little village of Baldoon, in southern Ontario. The curious events began in 1929, and at first showed all the classic signs of poltergeist activity: lumps of timber suddenly rose from the ground and hurled themselves around McDonald's barn, and soon afterwards household objects flew from shelves in the farmhouse and smashed to pieces on the floor.

Then the hail of missiles started. The house was showered by clusters of small pebbles, narrowly missing members of the McDonald family. The terrified Mrs McDonald, convinced that the family was the target of some evil supernatural force, called the stones "witch balls", and it was as The Ontario Witch Balls that the case was to become famous in Canadian ghost lore.

Word about what was happening at the McDonald farm quickly spread, and people came from miles around to satisfy their curiosity. Most of them went away disappointed, having witnessed nothing out of the ordinary, but some claimed to have seen the flying stones for themselves. Others said that they had heard strange noises, whistlings and hummings, as though the air around the house was charged with some strange force.

The bombardments continued on and off for the next two years and the McDonalds grew steadily more depressed, shunning their friends and neighbours and driving off curious sightseers.

Mrs McDonald, still convinced that witchcraft was at the root of the whole affair, called in someone who purported to be a witchfinder in a desperate bid to exorcise the phenomenon. Nothing worked. Then, in 1831, the attacks ceased as suddenly and mysteriously as they had begun.

For the McDonalds, life returned to normal – or as normal as it could be, after what they had experienced.

● BELOW Excavating a Roman villa site in France. The Romans often built their impressive structures on the sites of more ancient ruins – perhaps disturbing the spirits of long-dead Celtic people?

In 1979, five houses in Thornton Road, Birmingham, were suddenly subjected to regular assaults by flying stones. The residents were forced to board up their windows and erect screens of chicken wire to protect their property against the missiles. The police were called in and spent about 3,500 fruitless hours on the investigation up to the end of 1982, when the attacks ceased. Officers kept the houses under surveillance, using the latest equipment such as night-sights, image intensifiers and infra-red video, but although they were present when deluges of stones struck the houses, they were unable to establish where the missiles were coming from. The stones themselves were subjected to a thorough examination; there were no fingerprints on them, nor were there any traces of soil.

There was no doubt about the source of a large, round stone that crashed through the window of a mill in Cumbria, northern England, one day in 1887. It was still wet, and had come from the bed of the adjacent River Eden.

Bombardments of sound

There have been thousands of similar instances throughout the world. Sometimes, the "attacks" are accompanied by fearsome noises. In the early hours of Christmas Day, 1964, the people of Warminster, in Wiltshire, were roused abruptly from their slumbers by strange, frightening noises above the rooftops. There were crashes, thuds and clatters, as though the houses were being bombarded with giant rocks – and in the background was a high-pitched hum, vibrating in the frosty air. But outside, in the darkness, there was nothing to be seen, even though stone walls were shaking with the echoing vibrations. Suddenly, the noises stopped. Puzzled and not a little alarmed, the townspeople went back to bed.

● **BELOW A burial mount at Alton Priors, Wiltshire. Strange phenomena have often been seen and heard in the vicinity of such mounds, known as "barrows", where Celtic chieftains were laid to rest.**

Some were inclined to blame the Army; there was a big military camp near Warminster. But the Army did not usually carry out exercises on Christmas morning, and the mysterious sounds had not remotely resembled explosions. In fact, the Army was just as mystified. Nearby, where troops of the

1st Welsh Regiment were quartered, the guard had been turned out as soon as the first strange thunderclaps of sound were heard. Fully armed, the soldiers searched the barracks for intruders, but found no one. Then the noise – like hundreds of bricks falling on tin roofs – died away, and the soldiers returned to the guardroom, utterly perplexed.

At about the same time – shortly after six o'clock – a local woman was on her way to Holy Communion when she heard what sounded like dozens of gigantic wings rustling in the darkness above her head. Then the vibrations started – vicious, intense vibrations that pounded her and seemed to pierce into her brain. Her whole body felt as if it were encased in ice, while her head was seized by an unseen vice and squeezed relentlessly. Somehow, almost out of her mind with fear and virtually paralysed by the crushing pressure from above, she managed to stagger the last few steps up the hill to the church. As she collapsed in the church doorway, the pressure lifted and the vibrations ceased.

Altogether, the mysterious sonic bombardments lasted for six hours on that memorable Christmas morning. None of the people who experienced them – and there were many – could give a satisfactory explanation. The noises seemed to have died away – it was hoped for good.

Then, on a cold February day in 1965, another weird sound split the air over Warminster – a vibrant, high-pitched hum that seemed to come from nowhere out of a clear sky. Its effect on a flock of pigeons flying nearby was catastrophic. The whole flock staggered in mid-air as though struck by a giant hand, and then the birds' small bodies plummeted to earth among the trees.

● The castle moat (right) and well (opposite, top) at Kronborg, Elsinore, are haunted by strange noises. This site, in Denmark, was made famous in William Shakespeare's tragedy, *Hamlet*.

Two witnesses, one of them a doctor, had seen the birds fall. Astonished, they ran to the spot and found the pigeons lying stone dead on the ground. There were no marks on their bodies; it was as though they had been paralysed in full flight by some unseen force.

The mysterious death of the pigeons marked the start of a fresh series of assaults by the "thing", and this time the attacks took a vicious turn. One person who felt their full fury was a 19-year-old joiner, plodding homewards along a pitch-dark, deserted road after seeing his girlfriend safely home. The night was silent; all sound was blanketed by a dense fog. At first, the joiner did not take much notice of a faint humming noise – but then it swelled into a shrill, ear-splitting screech as though all the devils in hell had been let loose.

Suddenly, a fearsome, bone-crushing pressure clamped down on the young man, forcing him to his knees in the road. An icy, stinging wind tore at his face, and noiseless waves of something inexplicable buffeted at his body. His head felt as though it were held in iron clamps, and with this sensation came a stark, sickly fear that turned his bones to jelly. Then the pressure lifted, leaving him free to grope his way home. His parents took one look at his white face and terrified eyes and sent for the doctor, who treated the young man for severe shock.

Animals suffered most of all from the "thing's" assaults, presumably because their brains were more finely attuned to the ultrasonic vibrations that emanated from it. After one weird burst of ultrasound, dozens of field mice were found lying dead, their fur strangely singed and their bodies perforated with tiny holes. Dogs and cats became violently ill, while canaries and budgerigars toppled dead from their perches.

The violent sound-attacks lasted until the end of June 1965. Hordes of scientists and government investigators descended on Warminster and the surrounding district to study the phenomenon – and came away baffled. All sorts of theories were put forward, Unidentified Flying Object activity being prominent among them.

But Wiltshire is an ancient county. Here, Celtic tribes made their hill forts, dug long barrows for their dead, and practised rituals of which we know nothing. With their deep awareness of the forces of nature, they manipulated the elements that surrounded them with skills and secrets that have long since been lost to us. Is it possible that their priests unleashed forces that were uncontrollable – supernatural forces that from time to time gather their power and break out in violent demonstration? And is it possible that whatever forces produced the Warminster phenomenon are the same as those that plagued Gilbert Smith, and George Walton, and thousands of others like them all over the world?

Someday, perhaps, science may provide an answer.

The Bell Witch

But could science provide an answer to the phenomenon known as the Bell Witch, which made life thoroughly miserable for farmer John Bell in 1817 and for several years afterwards? It is doubtful.

John Bell lived in an isolated farmhouse in Robertson County, Tennessee, with his wife, four sons and one daughter. A few slaves were also quartered in some outhouses. In this instance, too, the mysterious events began with what would nowadays be associated with poltergeist activity: rappings, scratchings and other odd noises, followed by physical manifestations. Bed coverings would be pulled off, members of the family would be slapped across the face by an invisible hand, and so on.

At first, the Bells tried to keep the odd goings-on a secret, but after a while they became so distraught that this was no longer possible. The worst-afflicted member of the family was John Bell's daughter Elizabeth, known as Betsy, who was 12 years old at the time. It seemed as though the "thing" bore a special grudge against her.

At last, in desperation, John Bell turned to an old and trusted friend for help. Neighbour James Johnson was renowned for his piety; he was a lay preacher, and much respected in the community. Johnson quickly established that no hoax was involved, and made frequent visits to the Bell farm to try and establish contact with the thing.

After a while, it became apparent that whatever was haunting the Bell house was trying to speak. According to one account:

It commenced whistling when spoken to, in a low, broken sound, as if trying to speak in a whistling voice, and in this way progressed, developing until the whistling sound was changed to a weak, fluttering whisper uttering indistinct words. The voice, however, gradually gained strength in articulating and soon the utterances became distinct in a low whisper so as to be understood in the absence of any other noise.

Now that the thing could talk, it seemed eager to answer questions, although all the answers it gave were contradictory. In a loud, shrieking voice, it said, for example, that it was "... a spirit from everywhere, Heaven, Hell and the Earth. I'm in the air, in houses, any place at any time. I've been created millions of years ago. That is all I will tell you."

Another time it claimed that it was the spirit of someone who lay buried in the woods nearby, and on another occasion it said that it was the spirit of an early immigrant who had buried some treasure in the vicinity of the farmhouse and who had died before he could reclaim it. But the explanation that caught the attention of local people was that it was "nothing more nor less than old Kate Batts, witch". This caused problems, for Kate Batts, notorious for being a spiteful, foul-mouthed old hag, was very much alive. It seems that the people of Robertson County dismissed this claim, because they left Kate Batts alone.

For the Bell family, the torment went on for three years. Hardly a day passed without the "witch" shrieking around the house, but no apparition was ever seen. In the end, the strain began to tell on John Bell; his health failed, and he died on 20 December, 1820. The "witch" seemed to be delighted. At Bell's funeral, the air was filled with loud, unearthly shouts and snatches of song.

After John Bell's death the hauntings gradually died away. Eventually, after several months, the weird noises ceased altogether – leaving behind one of ghost lore's classic mysteries.

● **OPPOSITE TOP**
Hadrian's Wall, built by the Romans to separate Caledonia from the rest of Britain, is one of the most impressive monuments in the world. Over the centuries, there have been reports of stones from the wall moving mysteriously from their places.

● **OPPOSITE BELOW**
The splendid Norman castle at Richmond, North Yorkshire in the north of England, is haunted by a ghostly drum. Legend has it that centuries ago, a drummer boy was sent underground to follow a secret passage leading from the castle to Easby Abbey, two miles (3km) away, beating his drum so that others could follow on the surface. At the halfway point the drum-beat suddenly ceased, and the drummer boy was seen no more ...

The Californian gold-mining ghost town of Bodie

● BELOW The interiors of the buildings, left in a state of "arrested decay", create an eerie atmosphere, steeped in history.

● BOTTOM A view of the haunted International Order of Odd Fellows buildings.

The gold-mining ghost town Bodie, in California, is probably the finest preserved ghost town in the United States, being neither altered nor improved since it was deserted. Gold was discovered there in 1859 by Waterman S. Body (also known as William S. Bodey) and as a result had become home to around ten thousand people by 1879. The town was considered the worst of its kind for killings, robberies, stage holdups and godlessness – the Reverend FM Warrington labelled it in 1881 as "a sea of sin, lashed by the tempests of lust and passion."

The town stands now just as the last miners and townspeople left it abandoned in the 1930s, and was designated a state historic park in 1962. In its state of "arrested decay" the town attracts many visitors and some have been privy to more than a simple insight into the way of life of the former gold-seekers.

On one occasion, two photographers were photographing wall paper in an upstairs room in the International Order of Odd Fellows buildings, which had been used as the theatre, the Catholic Church, the Protestant Church and general meeting hall during the 1880s. One photographer remarked, "Oh, isn't this the building that is haunted?", whereupon there was a loud bang, and the floor began to vibrate. She quite spontaneously exclaimed, "Excuse me, no offense meant!", and the floor stopped shaking. Her companion had heard and felt nothing. A short while later they were both in an adjacent room photographing on different sides of the room, when something strange happened to their equipment. They found they could only photograph one side of the room; hence one photographer's camera stopped working when she tried to photograph some old wallpaper, but worked when she wanted to photograph the opposite wall, whereas her companion's camera would only shoot the wallpaper. The ghosts were playing games with them.

Another strange incident involving photography concerns the Cain family house, which is now the park headquarters. The house has a glass front enclosure and, as glass was rather difficult to come by at that time, this naturally attracts many photographers. As the story goes, a photography class was taking shots of the windows of the Cain house, but when the films had been developed, the instructor noticed that his photographs of the house, regardless of their location on the roll of film, had not been exposed. He checked the films of his students and discovered that not a single photograph of the Cain house had come out on any of their films. The mystery is still unexplained.

● LEFT The undertaker was never out of work in Bodie. The numerous and beautiful gravestones bear grim testimony to the often violent manner in which those who lie under them met their deaths.

● BELOW The JS Cain house, where ghost-like images have shown up on visitors' photos of the house, or else their films have remained black when developed.

On another occasion two people were sitting near the opening of a mining pit, while casually tossing pebbles down the shaft and listening out if any hit the bottom. Suddenly they heard the words "Stop that!", but not sure if they had heard correctly, they continued tossing the pebbles. Again they were loudly reprimanded with "Stop that!" Suitably unnerved, they promptly did just that, and are now firm believers in ghosts.

● RIGHT Bodie's houses are full of original artifacts. These evoke vivid images in the minds of modern-day visitors.

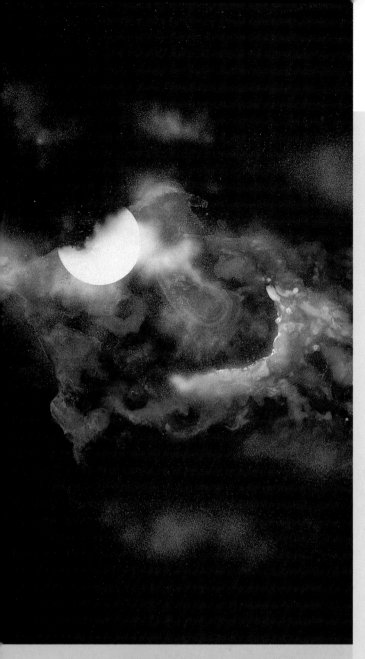

Ghostly Lights and Ghostly Ladies

Twenty miles (32 km) south-east of Galway Bay, in Ireland's lovely County Clare, lies the village of Crusheen. As you drive along the N18 route leading from Galway to Limerick, you could pass it by and hardly notice its cluster of whitewashed houses.

Following that same road southwards, two miles (3 km) further on, you come to the northern shore of Lough Inse Chronain – Lake Inchicronan. During the spring and summer months, you can cross over a rocky causeway to reach the small, barren island that lies in the centre of the lake. In winter, the causeway is often completely submerged.

On the island stand the ruins of Inchicronan Abbey, and nearby is the cemetery where the villagers of Crusheen have been laid to rest for centuries. By day it is a peaceful place, where tourists often stop for a while before going in through Ennis, Limerick and the River Shannon. But no inhabitant of Crusheen will venture near Inchicronan after dark, for in western Ireland old superstitions die hard – and the lake is linked with the village in a weird legend that defies any attempt at rational explanation.

According to Irish folklore, an impending death is said to be heralded by the appearance of the Banshee – the ghostly witch-woman who wails around the home of the doomed person in the darkness. But in Crusheen, the legend is different. When someone is about to die, the story goes, a

● BELOW Caerphilly Castle, in Wales, is said to be haunted by a green lady. She appears in daylight, walking the ramparts. The lady is thought by some to be Isabella, the estranged queen of King Edward II.

pair of mysterious lights – looking like candle flames – appear above the island in the lake. Slowly, at a height of six feet (1.8 m) or so above the ground, they move along the causeway and then along the road towards the village. Arriving at the home of the dying person, they float slowly up to rooftop height and remain there without moving for several minutes, before drifting back towards the lake and finally vanishing on the island.

On one occasion, when the strange lights appeared over a house in the village, the members of the family tried to dismiss the incident as superstitious nonsense. The next morning, one of them was killed in a car crash on his way to work. Another time, two men were wildfowling near the lake when they saw the lights appear on the island. But this time the lights moved eastwards, away from the village.

The next morning, the two men told the villagers what they had seen. The people of Crusheen were puzzled; as far as they knew, there was no one living in the direction taken by the lights. Then someone remembered Joe Cavan, an elderly hermit who lived in a hut a few miles away, not far from the eastern bank of Lake Inchicronan. Cavan used to visit the village once a week, to collect a few groceries and some tobacco. But it was more than a week since anyone had seen him.

One of the villagers volunteered to cycle over to Cavan's place. When he arrived, he found the door of the hut securely locked from the inside. Unable to see anything through the grimy window, he cycled back to Crusheen and returned with the local policeman. Together, the two men succeeded in breaking down the door. Inside the hut, stretched out on the floor, they found Joe Cavan. He was dead.

According to the legend, the phantom lights can only foretell the death of someone whose ancestors are buried in the churchyard near Inchicronan Abbey. Centuries ago, the abbey was the home of a flourishing community of monks, and it was the act of one of these monks, according to local belief, that gave rise to the strange story of the island lights.

One winter's night, so the legend goes, a woman lay dying in Crusheen. Through a blinding snow-storm, her son trudged the two miles (3 km) to Inchicronan Abbey and begged one of the monks to come to his mother's bedside to administer the last rites. The monk refused, saying that there would be time enough to make the journey in the morning, when the weather had cleared. But the woman died during the night, her sins unconfessed and unabsolved. And when the monk died, as a punishment for having failed in his duty, his spirit was doomed to wander beside that of the woman throughout eternity as a perpetual messenger of death.

The spirit of another unfortunate woman also seems condemned to wander the earth through eternity; at least, she has been seen at intervals for the past three centuries, and shows no sign of being laid to rest. She haunts Bramshill House at Hartney Wintney in Hampshire, southern England, which was once a stately home and is now a police training establishment.

The ghost, so the story goes, is that of a young, vivacious woman who was married on Christmas Day in 1725. After the wedding and the subsequent celebrations, the guests played party games. The young bride suggested hide and seek, and amid great merriment everyone spread out through the house.

Still carrying her wedding bouquet, the bride found herself in a remote and deserted part of the house. In a corridor, she came upon a beautifully carved oak chest – it can still be seen in the house today – and decided that it would make a perfect hiding place. It did, but in a horrible way she had not expected. The lid of the chest had a spring lock that snapped shut as she lay inside, hopelessly trapping her. It was 50 years before her contorted, mummified body was found. Scratch marks on the inside of the chest bore mute witness to the agony she must have endured before she succumbed to suffocation.

Her ghost has been seen many times, sometimes by distinguished guests of Bramshill House; King Michael and Queen Maria of Romania, who lived there with their children for some time after World War II, claimed to have seen the apparition on several occasions. She appears in different parts of the house, sometimes sitting in a chair, sometimes standing beside someone's bed, but always with an infinitely sad expression on her face. And always, when her image fades, she leaves behind her the scent of lilies-of-the-valley, the flowers that formed her bouquet so long ago, when the joy of her wedding day turned to horror.

The "Spook Lights" of Silver Cliff

Phantom lights are a phenomenon long associated with hauntings all over the world, and the United States is no exception. "Spook Lights", as they are called in the USA, usually appear in certain well-defined areas. One of the best known is in the West Mountain Valley area of Colorado, where the lights appear and hover over a graveyard that lies just outside the town of Silver Cliff. The place is now little more than a ghost town, one of many that sprang up during the mining boom of the nineteenth century and subsequently faded into obscurity as the silver mines were worked out.

In the 1880s, Silver Cliff was a rough, tough and thriving mining community with a population of about 5,000. One night a group of miners, considerably the worse for drink, told how they had witnessed mysterious lights hovering above the local graveyard. Their story was scorned at first, but then other, more sober observers began noticing the lights, and they have been seen at intervals over the years ever since.

In 1967 *The New York Times* picked up the story, and from then on Silver Cliff was frequently visited by ghost-hunters and others interested in occult phenomena. The story was sufficiently intriguing to attract the attention of the prestigious *National Geographic* magazine, which published an indepth article about the lights in 1969. This resulted from a visit by one of the magazine's representatives, Edward J. Linehan, who visited the graveyard in the company of a local resident named Bill Kleine.

In the darkness, both men saw round spots of blue-white light glowing dimly above the graves. As the two men approached, the lights drifted away; it was rather like chasing the end of a rainbow. Linehan reported that he pursued the lights for about fifteen minutes, and was completely unable to put forward a rational explanation for their presence. One theory was that they were caused by the presence of radioactive ore, but when the area was checked out with a Geiger counter there was no evidence of radiation above the normal background levels. Another theory, that the lights were reflections of some kind, was also dismissed when it was discovered that they were often seen shining in thick fog.

The more superstitious of Silver Cliff's inhabitants believe that the lights are the helmet lamps of long-dead miners, still searching for silver. Another theory is that they are "dancing blue spirits", long associated in American folklore with the burial grounds of the Cheyenne and Plains Indians, who interred their dead on sacred hilltops.

Whatever the true facts may be, the Silver Cliff lights have an interesting parallel thousands of miles away, on the other side of the Atlantic.

Royal ghosts and tragic queens

The bloodthirsty activities of King Henry VIII were responsible for the wanderings of a number of restless female spirits, mostly his decapitated wives.

One of them was the unhappy Anne Boleyn (her real name was Anne Bullen; it was changed to "Boleyn" because the latter sounded more aristocratic) haunts the Tower of London. Henry annulled his marriage to Catherine of Aragon in order to marry Anne, who was the queen's maid of honour; the act widened the growing rift between Henry and the Pope and led to Henry establishing himself as Head of the Church in England.

Anne's tenure as Henry's queen lasted only three years. A new face caught Henry's eye – that

● LEFT Henry VIII. His libidinous unruly urges led to the untimely death of several of his wives. The ghosts of some haunt Hampton Court.

● BELOW The site of the execution block in the Tower of London. One of history's most blood-stained plots of land, it is the scene of many hauntings. It was here that several of Henry VIII's wives met an untimely end.

of Jane Seymour – and Anne was gradually pushed into the background. Her enemies took advantage of this, and plied the king with evil stories about her; she was tried on a charge of infidelity, and was beheaded on 19 May, 1536.

Over the centuries, the ghost of Anne Boleyn has been seen wandering outside the little chapel where she spent the last night of her life. Strange lights have been witnessed inside the chapel itself; one sentry who peered inside swore that he had seen a ghostly procession of lords and ladies in Tudor dress, led by what was presumably Anne's headless ghost, proceeding slowly up the aisle and vanishing when it reached the altar.

The spirit of Jane Seymour, who succeeded Anne Boleyn in Henry's bed on the day after Anne's execution, roams Hampton Court. She died of puerperal fever in 1537 after giving birth to Henry's son and heir Edward, a sickly child. He was born on 12 October, 1537, and on the anniversary of his birth the ghost of Jane, dressed in white and carrying a lighted candle, ascends the staircase leading to Hampton Court Palace's Silver Stick Gallery, through which she drifts in a halo of light until she vanishes.

Her son was crowned Edward VI on the death of Henry in 1547, but only lived until the age of sixteen. At this time England was effectively ruled by the Duke of Northumberland, and on his orders the youthful Lady Jane Grey was proclaimed queen. She was ousted by Mary, the daughter of Catherine of Aragon, and reigned only nine days before being executed in the Tower. Lady Jane Grey's ghost has been seen on a number of occasions on the anniversary of her execution, sometimes running along the battlements.

The ghost of another of Henry VIII's wives was Katherine Howard, a granddaughter of the second Duke of Norfolk, who married Henry in 1541. The king doted on her, believing her to be chaste and virtuous. What he did not know was that, during Katherine's youthful years in the household of the

Duchess of Norfolk, she had indulged in a series of passionate affairs with young men.

For about a year and a half she used her considerable sexual experience to keep Henry happy, but then he discovered she was having an affair with her cousin, Thomas Culpepper. That in itself was a treasonable offence, but when the king learned of his wife's previous indiscretions her road to the block was swift. Arrested at Hampton Court, she broke free of her captors and dashed along a gallery to the chapel, where Henry, having just signed her death warrant, was weeping at his grievous loss and praying for her soul.

Screaming and crying, the distraught woman begged him to spare her life, but he ignored her entreaties. Shrieking, she was dragged away, placed on a barge and taken down the Thames to the Tower of London, where she was beheaded on 15 February 1542.

● **ABOVE AND BELOW** Hampton Court Palace, where the ghost of Katherine Howard runs screaming through the corridors, still pleading in vain for Henry VIII to spare her life. Unlike some of his queens, who met their end with dignity, she was dragged shrieking to the block.

● LEFT Lady Jane Seymour, the third of Henry VIII's wives, and the only one to provide him with an heir to the throne. Jane died shortly after giving birth and her son, Edward VI, lived only 16 years. On the anniversary of his birth, she drifts in a halo of light through Hampton Court Palace's Silver Stick Gallery, dressed in white and holding a lighted candle.

Today, she is one of the more celebrated ghosts of Hampton Court. From time to time, her spectre may be seen running along the gallery towards the chapel, howling terribly. At one time late in the 19th century, things got so bad that the gallery was closed and used as a storage space for furniture and tapestries. It was reopened to the public in 1918 and Katherine's ghost is still seen periodically, most often in the gallery but also in the gardens of Hampton Court.

One of the most prolific royal ghosts is that of Mary, Queen of Scots, who was kept under house arrest in various castles by England's Queen Elizabeth I before being beheaded at Fotheringay Castle, Northamptonshire, on 8 February 1587. When the castle was demolished upon the orders of King James I at the beginning of the 17th century, some of its fittings were purchased by William Whitwell, landlord of the Tabret Inn.

Among the interior fittings that were bought by Whitwell was an oaken staircase which Mary had walked down to face her executioner in one of the halls of Fotheringay Castle. It is said that her spectre has been seen and heard still walking down it, accompanied by the sound of mysterious footfalls and a sudden drop in temperature, a phenomenon often associated with the appearance of ghosts.

Another place where Mary's ghost appears from time to time is the Turret House, which forms part of the old manor castle at Sheffield, in Yorkshire. Mary spent about 14 years as a prisoner in Sheffield Castle, from 1570 to 1584 and most of that time was spent in the Turret House. Originally built as a porter's lodge, the Turret House was small, and therefore Mary could be more easily guarded. She had a great many Catholic sympathizers who were eager to see her on the throne of England in place of Elizabeth, and they were constantly planning ways for her to escape. For many years her ghost was seen, dressed all in black and gliding from one room to another in the Turret House, which today stands derelict.

The stately homes of England abound in female ghosts, not all of them particularly pleasant. For example, the old hall at Burton Agnes in the north of England is haunted by a troublesome being known to the locals as "Old Nance". She was the youngest daughter of Sir Henry Griffiths, who built the hall in 1600 or thereabouts.

One night, Anne Griffiths was mortally wounded – some say by thieves – as she returned home from a visit to friends. As she lay dying, she made her sisters promise to cut off her head and bury it deep inside one of the walls of the house she loved so much. The sisters promised to do as she wished,

● **BELOW LEFT** Mary, Queen of Scots, is the most prolific of the royal ghosts. She has been seen in several of the stately homes where she was kept under arrest by Queen Elizabeth I of England.

● **BELOW RIGHT** Fotheringay Castle, where Mary, Queen of Scots, was beheaded. A staircase from the castle was bought by the landlord of an inn at nearby Oundle, and Mary's ghost has appeared on it from time to time. She walked down this staircase to meet her fate.

but they were secretly horrified by the suggestion and had no intention of carrying it out. Anne was buried, head and all.

Soon afterwards, strange things started to happen in Burton Agnes Hall. Doors slammed, mysterious crashes rocked the house, and hideous groans were heard, accompanied by the sound of running footsteps. Terrified, recalling Anne's dying wish, her sisters sought the advice of the local vicar, who agreed to have the coffin exhumed.

When the coffin was opened, the horrified on-lookers found that Anne's head – already a skull with no trace of flesh on it – had already been severed from the rest of the body. It was taken back to the hall and kept in various convenient niches, mostly where nobody could see it. Over the years, succeeding owners of the hall tried to get rid of it, always with dire consequences. For many years the skull was kept on a table in the Great Hall, but then someone had it bricked up in a wall. It is still there today – but the ghost of Anne Griffiths continues to slam a door from time to time and let out an occasional groan, just to remind people that she's still around.

MARIE · STVART · REYNE · DESCOSSE
VEVFE · DE · FRANCOIS · SECOND

● ABOVE Ghostly ladies from France. These pictures show the ghost of a black lady terrifying courtiers, and the spirit of a dead wife arising from her body as mourners look on.

The fate of the *Palatine*

One tale from America combines a ghostly light with a ghostly lady. The story of the Palatine Light concerns a Dutch ship, the *Palatine*, which set sail for Philadelphia in the winter of 1752, laden with immigrants bound for the New World. As the vessel approached the coast of North America, disaster struck. A series of fierce storms swept in from the Atlantic, and by the time they had blown themselves out the ship had been reduced to little more than a battered hulk.

For the terrified passengers, the nightmare was only just beginning. The crew of the *Palatine* mutinied, murdered their captain and ran amok. They stripped the terrified passengers of their valuables, savagely raped several of the women, and then made off in the lifeboats, leaving the passengers to their fate. Some hours later the ship, which by then was beginning to sink, ran aground on Block Island off the coast of Rhode Island, a

place made notorious by a gang of brigands known as the Block Island Wreckers. Their speciality was to lure vessels on to the rocks, plunder them and murder everyone on board.

On this occasion, the Wreckers took pity on the luckless passengers of the *Palatine* and brought them safely ashore. But one woman steadfastly refused to leave the ship, even after the Wreckers set it on fire. She had been driven insane by the horrors she had endured, and she now clung to the stump of a shattered mast, shrieking horribly as the blazing vessel drifted out to sea.

It is said that, on certain nights, the phantom light of the *Palatine* may still be seen, drifting offshore until it is extinguished in the darkness, accompanied by the woman's heart-rending screams. No one can say how much of the story is true, but the Palatine Light is certainly one of the best-known ghostly legends of America's North Atlantic islands.

Lost Lovers

The revenge of Jeanne de Clisson

O n the banks of the River Loire, not far from Nantes, in Brittany, stands the small town of Clisson. It is dominated by an historic Norman castle, a fortress said to be haunted by the ghost of a beautiful young woman who, brutally torn from her husband, set out to wreak a terrible vengeance on his murderers.

The story begins in 1313, during the reign of King Philippe IV of France. His good looks earned him the nickname of Philippe the Fair, but his rule was a bloodthirsty one; by 1312 long wars against the Flemish had made his country virtually bankrupt, and in that year he suppressed the Order of the Knights Templar with great brutality in order to seize their considerable wealth.

Philippe dealt ruthlessly with any factions which presented, or were likely to present, a threat to his sovereignty. In particular, he kept a close watch on Brittany, whose Celtic population had strong racial ties with the people of Cornwall, and ordered his cousin, the Duke of Brittany, to report any suspects to him.

It was not long before the name of Count Olivier de Clisson came to Philippe's notice. De Clisson owned a castle and enormous estates in Brittany,

● BELOW The French town of Clisson and its medieval castle. The fortress is haunted by the ghost of a beautiful young woman who exacted a terrible revenge on those responsible for the death of her husband.

her father's castle on the mouth of the Loire, over-looking the sea. Her cup had been full. She had loved her husband dearly, and had looked forward to a serene, full life at his side. Now, at one blow, her hopes and dreams were shattered forever.

For a month Jeanne de Clisson mourned her husband, shutting herself away in the castle with her grief. When she finally emerged she rode all alone through her husband's lands, unsmiling and speaking to no one. Soon afterwards she began to sell the estates, until nothing remained but the castle; soon that too was deserted, for Jeanne moved into a rough fisherman's hut by the mouth of the Loire together with her two small sons and her chamberlain. Within a matter of months she had faded into obscurity; it was as though she had never existed.

Secretly, however, she had embarked on the first step along the trail of vengeance. Using the money she had earned from the sale of her estates, she fitted out three powerful warships in nearby Nantes. Her chamberlain scoured the more disreputable harbour taverns, recruiting tough, fearless seamen who would sell their souls for a gold coin.

One morning in the spring of 1314, the ships were gone. They had sailed during the night on the ebb tide. On the way down the Loire to the sea they paused briefly at a designated spot to pick up an unknown person who, the ships' captains had been told, would be their admiral. A few minutes later, the rough sailors stared in an open-mouthed aston-ishment as their new commander came aboard: for the admiral was a woman. It was Jeanne de Clisson, and with her came her two small sons.

A couple of weeks later, three exhausted sea-men struggled ashore on the coast of Brittany. They had been part of the crew of one of the King's ships, and they told a horrifying story of how, one night, three terrible vessels with black hulls and red sails had descended on them. All their comrades had been put to death; they alone had been spared and left to make their way ashore, to spread the word that Jeanne de Clisson's revenge had begun.

It was the start of a reign of terror that was to last for thirteen years. One ship after another fell victim to Jeanne's merciless seamen, and on more than one occasion the black-painted vessels sailed boldly into harbours and estuaries to destroy merchant ships lying at anchor. A few of their crew members were always left alive to tell the tale.

and was powerful enough to make no secret of the fact that he had many friends in England. Perhaps he was too complacent; perhaps he never even suspected that King Philippe's obsessed mind per-ceived him as a source of potential danger which had to be eliminated. At any rate, he saw nothing out of the ordinary in receiving a summons to attend the Duke of Brittany in Rennes; often, in the past, he had advised the Duke on administrative matters.

So, with no inkling of the tragedy that was about to befall him, de Clisson rose into Rennes. On arriving at the Duke's castle, he was seized and dragged before a tribunal. There, without being given a chance to answer the trumped-up charges against him, he was condemned to death, and on 2 August, 1313, he was beheaded in Rennes market-place.

Behind him, sorrowing in the mighty castle that now had no purpose, Olivier de Clisson left a beautiful wife, Jeanne, and two baby sons. A gentle girl of eighteen, Jeanne had married de Clisson two years earlier, after spending her childhood in

The lost lovers of Pisgah Mountain

North Carolina is rich in ghost stories and legends, many of them handed down over the years by word of mouth rather than in writing. One such story, concerning the lost lovers of Pisgah Mountain, would not be out of place in Emily Bronte's *Wuthering Heights*.

● **ABOVE** The wild mountain country of North Carolina, where Jim Stratton and his lover Mary Robinson vanished in a blizzard. The ghosts of the tragic couple still wander the hillsides.

The lovers involved were Jim Stratton and Mary Robinson. He was seventeen, she only fifteen when they began a secret courtship sometime around the turn of the century. Mary's father guarded his daughter with great jealousy and had forbidden Jim Stratton to see her, hence the secrecy. When he found out that he hadn't managed to prevent the clandestine courtship, he played the nastiest trick that one mountain country man could play on another: he told the revenue men that young Stratton was running a liquor still up in the hills.

The upshot was that the revenue men descended on Jim's still one day and started to smash it up. Jim came on the scene while they were still at it, and shot one of them dead. The others fled in panic.

Jim realized that he was now a man on the run. He sought the help of a widow, a woman who had been a close friend of his mother, and told her that he planned to escape from the area as quickly as possible, taking Mary Robinson with him. He asked the widow if she would fetch the local preacher while he col-

lected Mary, and she agreed. It was snowing heavily by the time Jim returned to the widow's cabin with Mary. The girl was frightened – word of what Jim had done had already spread, and the hunt for him was on.

The widow duly returned with the preacher, who luckily was a man not given to ask many questions. The widow gave her own wedding ring to Mary, and a quick marriage service was performed. No sooner was it completed than they heard the sound of dogs barking down the trail that led to the cabin. Quickly the widow ushered Jim and Mary out of the house through the back door and watched them as they disappeared into the gathering December darkness. They had escaped safely into the shelter of the trees by the time the sheriff's men reached the cabin.

The man-hunt for Jim Stratton and Mary Robinson went on for several more days, until the depth of snow made it impossible to carry on the search. It was resumed after the spring thaw, but with no result. In desperation, Mary Robinson's father put notices in the local newspaper produced in neighbouring Asheville, pleading for information on the whereabouts of his daughter, but all in vain. She and Jim Stratton had disappeared from the face of the earth. They were never seen again.

But every year, so the mountain folk say, at the time of the first snowfall, the shades of a man and woman appear on the mountainside where Jim and Mary vanished in the blizzard; she is standing, he kneeling at her feet, holding her hand as though proclaiming his love – or, perhaps, begging her forgiveness for having taken her to her death in the frozen wilderness.

The Lost Lovers of Pisgah Mountain is a tragic tale, for there were only losers; Mary's father himself died heartbroken shortly after her disappearance. But tragedy is a central feature of most ghostly love stories and as in a case dating back to medieval France, the tragedy is accompanied by a wronged woman's bitter thirst for revenge.

Sometimes, noblemen from the King's court were discovered on board captured vessels; these were killed by Jeanne herself, cut down by the deadly axe she wielded.

King Philippe only lived to see the start of Jeanne's vengeance; he died on 29 November 1314. He was succeeded by his eldest son, Louis X, who died in 1316. Philippe V, the next in line, reigned until his death in 1322; he was succeeded in turn by Charles IV, who died in 1328.

Charles was the last of Philippe's sons; Jeanne could rest at last. In November 1328, for the last time, her three black ships sailed out of the Channel mists towards the French coast, where their crews beached them. Jeanne bade farewell to her seamen, each of whom had amassed a small fortune during the long years of plunder, and then travelled to Nantes with her two sons, now grown into young men and hardened by their experiences. At Nantes, she and the boys went their separate ways: she towards the Spanish border, they to restore the Château Clisson.

No one knows what became of Jeanne de Clisson. According to local legend, her restless spirit is still to be seen from time to time, wandering the battlements of the castle. Sometimes she appears in defiant pose, gazing westwards down the Loire towards the open sea; at others, as a sad, grey figure, with head bowed as though still mourning the husband she lost – or perhaps in atonement for the souls of innocent sailors doomed because of her vengeance.

● **BELOW** The river adjacent to Goodrich Castle, in Herefordshire, is haunted by the ghosts of two lovers who tried to escape from the fortress when it was besieged by Oliver Cromwell's forces. The swollen waters of the River Wye claimed them both.

English castles and stately homes

Some English castles have their ghostly lovers, too. One is Goodrich Castle overlooking the River Wye in Herefordshire. Once a vital strongpoint on the Welsh Borders, it was held by a man named Clifford during the English Civil War and was besieged by part of Oliver Cromwell's army led by Colonel Birch in 1646. Birch had a problem in that his niece Alice, who accompanied him, was in love with Clifford.

At some point during the siege she fled from her uncle's side and managed to get inside the castle, where she joined her lover. Undeterred by her presence inside Goodrich, Colonel Birch continued with the siege and began to batter the castle with heavy mortars. Realizing that it was only a question of time before the fortress fell, Clifford and Alice, mounted on one horse, slipped away under cover of darkness and tried to cross the river. Its waters were swollen by a recent storm and they were swept away; their bodies were never found.

Sometimes, on stormy nights, witnesses have seen a phantom horseman with a lady mounted behind him, both wearing clothing of Cromwell's day, entering the waters of the Wye near Goodrich Castle, only to disappear mysteriously.

Another ghostly lover, who has haunted Raynham Hall, a stately home in East Anglia, England, is thought to be the spirit of Dorothy Walpole, sister of one of England's Prime Ministers, Sir

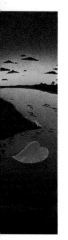

● BELOW Raynham Hall in Norfolk is haunted by the ghost of Dorothy Walpole, sister of one of England's Prime Ministers. According to the official version she died of smallpox, but in reality she may have been murdered by her husband, Charles Townshend.

Robert Walpole. She was brought up alongside a boy named Charles Townshend, a viscount who was set to inherit a vast fortune and considerable estates.

Later, Dorothy and Charles fell in love and wanted to marry, but Dorothy's father refused permission on the grounds of his pride; he did not want the Townshends to think that his family coveted their fortunes. In the end, Charles married somebody else; Dorothy went to London and then to Paris, where she drowned her sorrows in reckless living.

When she learned that Charles's wife had died, however, she was soon on her way home to Raynham Hall. Within a year, she and Charles were married; it was 1712. For a time they were happy, until rumours of his new wife's escapades in Paris began to reach Charles's ears. He made inquiries, and learned that the rumours were true. In anger, he confined her to her room and would allow no one near her.

Within a short time, Dorothy was dead. According to the official records the cause was smallpox, which might have been the real reason why Charles placed her in quarantine, but according to some accounts she was quietly murdered.

● RIGHT The ghost of Raynham Hall. Is this Dorothy Walpole, or another spectre? Dorothy's demise was a direct result of the abandoned life she had led in Paris, details of which reached the ears of her jealous husband.

● ABOVE George III and his queen, Caroline, pictured at the garden entrance of St James's Palace. The king was reportedly terrified when, during a visit to Raynham Hall, Dorothy Walpole's ghost suddenly appeared at his bedside.

Whatever the reason behind her demise, her ghost began to appear. She was dressed in a brown robe, her hair dishevelled, her face grey and distressed.

On one occasion, in 1786, she terrified no lesser a person than King George III by appearing beside his bed; the story goes that he dashed around the hall in his nightgown, ordering everyone out of bed and vowing that he would not stay in the place another hour.

Witnesses who saw the ghost in subsequent years told how it seemed always to be grinning, and that there were only dark hollows where the eyes should

have been. Towards the end of the 19th century its appearances became fewer, until they dwindled away almost completely. But in 1936, she was seen by two photographers who had been commissioned to take pictures of Raynham Hall's interior. They saw a shadowy form suddenly materialize on the main staircase, and one of the men had the presence of mind to take a photograph of it.

When the plate was developed, it showed the outline of a woman in a veil and white bridal gown. Her features were not discernible. Was it the ghost of Dorothy Walpole – or that of Charles Townshend's first wife?

● RIGHT Swan Pool, in Gloucestershire, England, is haunted by the spectre of a young woman carrying a child in her arms. According to legend, she drowned herself and the infant after being abandoned by the child's father – probably one of the local gentry.

Divided by faith – forbidden lovers

Nuns and monks feature prominently in the ghostly lovers' scenario, because in medieval times neither were as chaste as they are today. One place, not far from the famous Battle of Britain airfield at Kenley, Surrey, is haunted by the sorrowful figure of what appears to be a phantom nun. Sometimes, she is seen holding in her arms a bundle that could represent a child.

The nun starts her ghostly walks in a housing estate built on the site of a medieval village. This was excavated before the estate was built, and the remains of a chapel were found, together with an adjacent graveyard. The nun leaves behind her an aroma of what might be incense, and sometimes appears in broad daylight as well as at night.

In Guildford, a multi-storey car park in York Road is haunted by the tragic spectre of a tall, grey-eyed girl dressed in long robes of similar colour. Her hair is light auburn, tucked up under a cap. She is supposed to be the ghost of a 19-year-old Quaker girl called Lorna, who died under tragic circumstances 200 years ago after her father had threatened to throw her out of the house. Her "crime" was that she had fallen in love with a young man who was not a Quaker. Distraught, she ran from her home and, doubtless blinded by tears, fell to her death down a nearby quarry.

One sorrowful ghost, that of Dorothy, the daughter of Sir John Southworth, haunts Samlesbury Hall, a 14th-century manor house in Lancashire, England. In the 16th century, she fell in love with the son of a neighbouring family, the Hoghtons; the problem was that she was a Catholic and he a Protestant. Her brother, enraged by the thought that she was prepared to abandon what he considered to be the true faith, murdered her lover and buried him beside one of the hall's foundation walls (a male skeleton was, in fact, found there earlier this century). The luckless girl was packed off to a convent, where she quickly died of a broken heart. Her ghost appears at dusk, haunting the spot where her lover was killed.

The waterways of East Anglia are famous for the ghosts of tragic lovers. One of them is Horsey Mere, in Norfolk, England, once a trysting place for two young people from neighbouring villages; the young man, a farm worker, used to cross over in a boat to meet his girlfriend. One night, the boat overturned and he was drowned. His shade can be seen wandering the shore in despair, seeking his long-dead love.

● FAR RIGHT The waterways of East Anglia have numerous ghosts. Horsey Mere, in Norfolk, is haunted by the spirit of a young lover who drowned when his boat overturned as he was on his way to visit his girl in a nearby village.

Ghostly Tales of Terror

The story of "Black Aggie"

In the Druid Ridge Cemetery at Pikeville, outside Baltimore, Maryland, there lies the grave of American newspaper publisher, General Felix Angus, who died in the 1920s. His last resting place used to be marked by a strange and rather sinister-looking monument, commissioned by his family. It is no longer there, for reasons which will become clear.

The tombstone erected over the grave, designed by a well-known sculptor, featured a small black angel mounted on top. It became a prominent landmark in the cemetery, and acquired the somewhat irreverent nickname of "Black Aggie" among the people of Pikeville.

● **BELOW** A confrontation with death in a graveyard. Not unnaturally, many ghostly tales of terror are associated with burial grounds, where imagination and fear of the unknown can cause the mind to play strange tricks.

It also acquired a sinister reputation as newspapers reported a local tale that the black angel's eyes would glow red at the stroke of midnight. A terrifying legend grew around it; it was said that all the ghosts in the graveyard would assemble around the black angel at midnight, and that any human being unlucky enough to meet her glowing gaze would be instantly struck blind. No grass would grow in the shadow of the stone angel, and any pregnant woman foolish enough to stray that way would miscarry.

It all sounded like nonsense, but some members of a local college fraternity decided to put the story to the test as part of an initiation ceremony they dreamed up. A prospective candidate was required to spend the entire night sitting under Black Aggie. The story goes that the first candidate to take up the challenge was found dead at the foot of the tombstone the next morning. According to the autopsy, he had died of fright.

In 1962 there came a strange twist to the tale when one of Black Aggie's arms was found to be missing. The arm was later discovered in the trunk of a car belonging to a sheet metal worker, with a saw lying beside it. The man was sentenced to a term of imprisonment for desecrating a sacred monument, despite his rather ludicrous case for the defence: he claimed that Black Aggie had sawn off her own arm and presented it to him.

By this time, Black Aggie had become a tourist attraction. People would gather at the cemetery at midnight and stare at the statue in the rather fearful hope that they would actually see the angel's eyes start to glow in the dark. There were those, of course, who claimed that they had indeed witnessed this phenomenon, and had come away from it and not gone blind after all.

The attention being paid to the grave, with the threat of possible further desecration, was now a cause for serious concern in the Angus family. In 1967, they had Black Aggie removed and presented her to the Smithsonian Institution, which, perhaps wisely, did not put her on display.

The strange tale of Black Aggie might have had a tongue-in-cheek element about it; but there was nothing amusing about what happened to Englishman John Allen on what should have been a pleasant weekend's holiday.

● BELOW A young widow is visited by the ghost of her drowned husband. Many ghost stories have their origin in tragic drownings.

Horror in a French farmhouse

John Allen was cold, wet and thoroughly miserable. When he had set out from Calais at the start of that August weekend in 1951, his spirits had been high, and he had been looking forward to his cycling tour of France; but now, with a gash ripped in his front tyre by a piece of broken glass, in the middle of nowhere, several miles from the town of Angers, in Brittany, he was feeling far from happy. It was still daylight, but lowering clouds hung gloomily over the countryside and the rain lashed down in a steady sheet.

Allen had no spare inner tube with him, and after spending the best part of an hour trying to repair the damage, if only temporarily, he gave up in disgust and set out to push his bike to the nearest village. The road was lonely, deeply rutted and little better than a cart-track. For two hours he trudged on without seeing a living soul, becoming wetter and more miserable with every step.

At last, as he rounded a bend in the road, he saw a house. It was an impressive building, with tall

Margaret Leigh – the witch of St John's

In St John's Churchyard at Burslem, England, lies the grave of Margaret Leigh. It is more than 200 years old, and is notable for the fact that, while all the other headstones in the churchyard are orientated towards the east, this one faces west. Beneath it lie the remains of a woman who, according to local legend, was a witch – and whose spirit terrorized the good people of Burslem for some time after her death.

Margaret Leigh was born in 1680, the daughter of a well-respected yeoman family. As she grew older, she developed quite a remarkable ugliness – so much so, in fact, that the local parson, the Reverend Spencer, felt obliged to declare that she was a witch. She was lucky in that she was born too late to endure the witch-hunting fever that swept England in the mid-17th century, but nevertheless her parents felt obliged to turn her out of the family home. She went to live in an old cottage, kept a cow or two and made a living by selling milk.

The Reverend Spencer was still in office when Margaret died in April 1748. Immediately after the burial, the parson, who was a notorious drunkard, drank himself into a near stupor in the village inn and then set off to Margaret's cottage to see if there was anything of value he might appropriate.

Within minutes he was back in the inn, shaking and in a state of terror. Eventually, fortified by more drink, he gasped out his story. He had gone into the cottage to find a fire burning brightly in the grate; and there, sitting next to it, was Margaret Leigh, staring at him with an expression of utter malevolence.

His fellow-tipplers, well used to his drinking habits, laughed at him – but then the ghost of Margaret Leigh began to walk the village streets, howling. After a while, the villagers became so terrified of running into her that no one would venture outdoors after dark. It made no difference; Margaret began to appear in their houses, where she would sit knitting in a corner of the room. Eventually, the demand for action became so great that Parson Spencer, together with five other clergymen, performed an exorcism. The story goes that they lured the spirit of Margaret Leigh into a water-filled pig trough, which they had placed in the middle of St John's Church, and extinguished it.

● FAR LEFT Necromancers raising a corpse from the dead. The morbid fascination with resurrecting the dead in the 19th century gave rise to such works as Mary Shelley's novel *Frankenstein*.

● LEFT The original ghostly tale of terror from Charles Dickens' *A Christmas Carol*: the miserly Ebenezer Scrooge is visited by the spirit of his one-time partner Jacob Marley, who warns him of the consequences if Scrooge fails to mend his ways.

chimneys. As he drew nearer, Allen saw that it was a farmhouse, complete with outbuildings. It stood at the end of a long, overgrown drive; beyond it, the waters of a small lake danced and shivered under the onslaught of the raindrops.

Allen soon found that the house was deserted and dilapidated. The lower windows had been boarded up, but the front door was unlocked. He went inside, wrinkling his nose at the strong smell of decay. There was mould everywhere. But the furniture was still there, dotted with ugly, fungus-like growths. That was strange; he wondered why no one had removed it.

There was a fireplace in the living-room, and he decided to try and get a fire going. He dashed across the farmyard to one of the outbuildings and, after a few minutes' searching, uncovered an armful of firewood. Holding it under his coat to keep it dry, he ran back to the farmhouse. After arranging the sticks in the grate, he went out into the hall, where he had left his bicycle, and brought out his Primus stove, intending to sprinkle some paraffin on the wood.

Suddenly, a wave of inexplicable terror engulfed him. Running across the full length of the hall, between a French window and the door of the living room, a glistening wet trail showed up clearly against the thick carpet of dust. It was just as if someone had dragged a wet bundle into the house.

Allen stood absolutely still, peering into the shadows of the hall. Seeing no one, he went back into the room, bending over to inspect the floor. The wet trail crept across the room and ended at a mouldering sofa, on which lay a few tattered pieces of cloth. Allen had not noticed them before because of the poor light. Now, looking at them closely, he saw that they were the remains of a pair of pyjamas. Gingerly, he lifted them between his thumb and forefinger; they were falling apart from decay and were caked with dried mud. A sudden wave of nausea swept over him and he dropped the pyjamas hurriedly.

With a considerable effort, he pulled himself together. There was no reason for the fear that clutched him; he was a powerful man, quite capable of dealing with any hostile intruder. Nevertheless, he could not shake off the uneasy feeling that he wasn't alone. He did not relish the prospect of spending the night in the farmhouse, but on the other hand he had no intention of venturing outside

again while it was still raining.

It was now 5.30 pm. If the rain stopped in time, he might just be able to reach the nearest town before dark. Whistling to keep his spirits up, he set about lighting the fire. A welcome yellow flame curled around the sticks – only to be blown out again by a sudden draught.

It was then that Allen heard the noise – a soft, squashy sound, as though something large and sodden had fallen on the floor in the hall outside. Allen was on his feet in an instant, every nerve tense and a heavy poker in his hand. Moving silently to the door, he flung it open – but there was nobody in the hall, and the only sound was the steady swish of the rain. Allen closed the door and went back to relight the fire. A minute later, he heard the strange noise again.

ABOVE A midnight visitation in a French dungeon. This illustration is probably intended to show that, under such circumstances, it would be easy for the imagination to run riot.

This time, when he opened the door and looked out into the hall, he froze in horror. The damp track on the floor was a lot wetter, and it seemed to be inching its way towards him. Step by step he retreated into the room, gazing in open-mouthed fear as the wet trail crept across the threshold and moved slowly towards the sofa. It spread up the side of the sofa, creeping on until it reached the spot where the tattered pyjamas were lying.

Suddenly, the pyjamas began to twitch and jerk, as though invisible fingers were plucking at them – and a moment later, in front of Allen's horrified eyes, they began to swell and fill out as though in human shape. As they did so, water oozed from them.

Allen had had enough. He ran blindly out into the rain, not knowing or caring where he was going as long as it was away from that awful place. At last, utterly exhausted, he found himself outside a little inn about a mile up the road. People put down their drinks and stared in amazement as Allen reeled into the bar. Seeing the state the Englishman was in, the landlord pushed a glass of cognac into his hand without asking any questions. Thankfully, Allen gulped it down. Feeling a little better, he tried to make the landlord understand what had happened. One or two people in the inn spoke a few words of English, and nodded knowingly as they pieced his story together.

The landlord plied Allen with more drink and sent his wife off to prepare a room. Looking meaningfully at his customers, he told Allen that his bicycle and rucksack would be quite safe at the farm; no one would dream of going near the place. Allen wanted to know why, but the landlord just shook his head and the Englishman was too tired to press the matter. Gratefully, he climbed the stairs to his room, stripped off his wet clothes in front of the fire and was fast asleep within minutes.

The following morning, Allen once again raised the question of the deserted farm – and this time, with the aid of a few newspaper cuttings produced by the landlord, he was able to unearth the facts. They combined to make a terrible story.

During World War II, the farmhouse had been occupied by an artist named Marc Baus. He was a notorious collaborator, and in the course of the war he was directly responsible for the deaths of several Resistance fighters.

In 1946, Baus was arrested and brought to trial. He was found guilty, but the sentence was surprisingly light – a mere two years' imprisonment. He returned to the farmhouse in 1948, a sick man in constant fear of reprisals by people in the area who had lost friends and relatives because of his treachery. One night, a big crowd gathered outside the farmhouse; they screamed threats at Baus and

● **ABOVE** The castles of Wales have their share of ghosts. This one, brooding on the skyline at Dolwyddelan in Gwynned, was the birthplace of the Welsh prince Llywelyn the Great in 1173. His grandson, Llywelyn the Last, took part in the final struggle against Edward I of England before the castle was captured in 1283. His ghost is said to haunt the site.

hurled stones through the windows before they were dispersed by local police.

The next day, Baus had disappeared. At first, it was thought he had left the area, but two months later his partly decomposed body, clad in pyjamas, was found among the weeds in the shallow water of the little lake behind the farmhouse. When the police arrived, the body was carried into the house through the French windows and laid on the sofa in the living room, where the post-mortem examination took place. The cause of death had been drowning, either by accident or suicide; foul play was not suspected.

Allen learned that he was not the only person to undergo a terrifying experience in the old farmhouse. A year after Baus's death, two labourers sheltered in the house from a storm – only to run from the place in abject terror after seeing the phenomenon of the wet trail on the floor and the moving pyjamas.

The farmhouse is gone now, levelled to make way for a new autoroute. Perhaps the ghost of Marc Baus is gone too, exorcised at last by bulldozers.

● ABOVE A would-be grave robber is confronted by a dead man. In the late 18th century grave robbing was rife in Europe, fuelled by the desperate need of doctors to understand more about the nature of human anatomy.

● LEFT Prestbury in Gloucestershire, the most haunted village in England. Almost every other house has its ghost, and the Church of St Mary is haunted too.

The Laird of Inverawe

One of the best-known tales of ghostly terror concerns a Scot, Major Duncan Campbell, who one stormy night in 1747 inadvertently gave shelter to the murderer of his cousin, Donald Campbell. Donald's blood-soaked spectre appeared at the foot of Duncan's bed, pointing an accusing finger and whispering: "Inverawe, Inverawe, blood has been shed. Shield not the murderer."

Three times more the ghost of the dead man appeared. On the third occasion it whispered: "Farewell, Duncan Campbell. Farewell, until we meet again – at Ticonderoga."

The name meant nothing to Duncan Campbell. The vision did not appear again, and gradually the frightening experience faded from his memory. Years went by, and Major Duncan Campbell – a

● LEFT General Abercrombie, whose forces carried out the costly and fruitless assault on Fort Ticonderoga in North America on 8 July 1758. It was here that Major Duncan Campbell met the end that had been foretold by his murdered cousin, Donald Campbell.

professional soldier to his fingertips – rose to be second in command of the 42nd Regiment of Foot, the famous "Black Watch" regiment. In 1758, the Black Watch was sent to Britain's North American colonies to take part in the war against the French. The regiment marched northwards from Albany as part of a force under General Abercrombie, and set up camp beside Lake George. Abercrombie planned to launch an assault on Fort Carillon where the French were firmly entrenched.

Soon after the regiment's arrival, Major Duncan Campbell learned that Fort Carillon had an Indian name. It was Ticonderoga. And that same night, the vision of the murdered Donald Campbell appeared to him again – after more than ten years.

With Abercrombie's force was an historian named Parkman. Writing about the battle that was to come, he said: "There was Rogers with the Rangers and Gage with the Light Infantry, and the Highlanders of the Forty-Second with their Major, Duncan Campbell of Inverawe, silent and gloomy amid the general cheer, for his soul was dark with forebodings of death."

In his mind, Duncan Campbell was absolutely certain that he was going to die. On the morning of the battle, he told his fellow officers about the apparitions, and said quite calmly that he would die that day.

On 8 July, 1758, the British attacked Ticonderoga, but the French were ready for them. They had entrenched themselves firmly around the fort, and had built a barrier of pointed stakes in which the advancing British soldiers became hopelessly entangled. The carnage was fearful; the bodies of the British Redcoats piled up in heaps among the tangled undergrowth around the fort, but still they came on. After repeated and costly attacks, Abercrombie realized the futility of it all and ordered a general withdrawal to Lake George.

Duncan Campbell had been in the thick of the battle, fighting like a man possessed, as though anxious to meet his fate as quickly as possible. But although men dropped lifeless all around him, his only injury was a flesh wound in the arm from a musket ball.

It was as though the dark burden of ten years had suddenly lifted from his shoulders. Perhaps the ghost of his dead cousin had relented. Perhaps he was not destined to die in these American backwoods, after all.

But ten days later, he was dead. The wound in his arm had turned septic and gangrene had set in. An army surgeon amputated the limb, but it was useless. There was nothing he could do to save Campbell's life. Fate and the Laird of Inverawe had kept a long-delayed rendezvous.

Mad Myers of Berkeley Square

● BELOW Death comes to Earth. A terrifying illustration of the doom that hovers over mankind in one form or another.

London is not England's most haunted city; that dubious honour falls to York, where phantom Roman soldiers march through excavated parts of the old legionary fortress deep below York Minster. But many of London's ghosts inspire sheer terror in the minds of those who witness them.

The most famous haunted house in England's capital is No 50, Berkeley Square, which was once the home of Victorian Prime Minister George Canning. It is said that people have been driven mad – even frightened to death – by some spectral horror that lurks in an upstairs room there. The hauntings seem to have begun sometime in the 1830s, after a young woman hurled herself to her death from an upstairs window, and reached their peak 50 years later. This was after the house had been occupied for several years by a Mr Myers, a recluse who allegedly went mad after his fiancée ran off with another man. He had spent a small fortune furnishing the house to delight his bride; now he spent his days and nights wandering from room to room mourning his lost love, a melancholy figure who would have made a good bedfellow for Charles Dickens' Miss Faversham.

He died in 1878, and two years later No 50 Berkeley Square was bought by a family called Bentley. The elder daughter was engaged to an army officer, Captain Kenfield. One night in 1880 a housemaid was preparing a room for the captain, who was coming to stay, when her terrified screams tore through the house. The Bentleys rushed upstairs and found the girl in convulsions at the foot of the bed, an expression of unspeakable horror on her face. Unable to speak, she was rushed to St George's hospital, where she died the following day.

Captain Kenfield insisted on spending a night in the room, despite the pleas of his fiancée. He agreed that he would ring a bell if anything nasty happened. Sure enough, the bell sounded just after midnight, sending the Bentley family dashing upstairs once more. Captain Kenfield was lying on the floor, convulsed with terror, his staring eyes fixed on a corner of the room. He eventually recovered, but he was never the same man again – and he was never able to tell what he had seen.

After World War II, No 50 Berkeley Square was taken over by a firm of antique booksellers. Since then, there have been no reports of further hauntings – but perhaps Mad Myers is biding his time.

328 Chase Street

The events at No 50 Berkeley Square, however, seem almost insignificant compared to what went on for years at the home of Jack and Janet Smurl and their four daughters. Devout Roman Catholics, they shared a warm, loving family life, and when they moved into their new home at 328 Chase Street, West Pittston, Pennsylvania, on the first day of October 1973, their happiness seemed complete. The house stood in a quiet cul-de-sac, and in the Smurls' eyes was an ideal place in which to bring up four young children. They were soon to be proven horribly wrong.

It was in January 1974 that strange and terrifying things began to happen. First, stains appeared on the living-room carpet, and reappeared just as fast as the Smurls could clean them up. Deep scratch marks appeared on furniture. There were loud rapping sounds, as though someone was knocking hard on the walls and ceilings, and from time to time a foul, inexplicable stench pervaded the house. The telephone would ring, and go on ringing even when the receiver was lifted.

The phenomena continued in much the same vein for ten years. The Smurls, depending on their faith, endured them stoically, concluding that they were being put to the test by forces of evil. Then, early in 1985, those forces launched an all-out offensive against the entire family.

First, the voices started – whispering, insidious voices that came from nowhere, calling on the family members by name. Then the apparitions came, shadowy figures that seemed to be wearing old-fashioned clothing. They drifted through the rooms, always leaving behind a sense of chill foreboding. They seemed to be smiling, but the smiles were sinister, as though bearing a promise of worse to come.

There *was* worse to come. The Smurls began to be subjected to savage physical attacks out of nowhere, sometimes being knocked to the ground and dragged around the room. Jack and Janet had hideous nightmares in which they were subjected to sexual assaults by loathsome, corpse-like creatures. And the attacks were not confined to the house; they occurred even when the family was away on a camping holiday.

In the end, driven almost insane by the horrors they were enduring, the Smurls enlisted the power of the Church. A priest carried out an exorcism, but to no avail. The hauntings went on, and only ceased when the Smurls abandoned the house and fled to another part of Pennsylvania in 1987.

Why this particular family should have been subjected to such horrific attacks, over such a long period of time, remains a mystery. But the house at 328 Chase Street, like many others in West Pittston, was built over long-forgotten underground mine workings. Were the spectres that tormented the Smurls associated in some way with an old mining disaster, where trapped men gasped away their lives in terror, clutched by the freezing darkness deep beneath the surface?

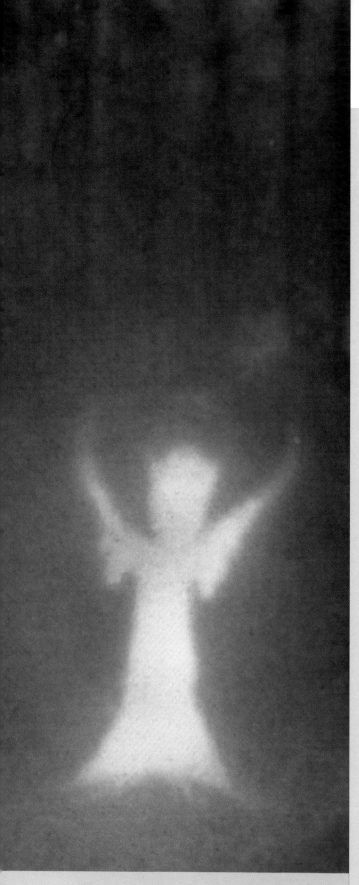

Friendly Ghosts

Esau Dillingham – the "Smoker" of Labrador

The blizzard screamed down from the east without warning, raging across the lonely, snow-covered hills of Labrador. It caught two Royal Canadian Mounted Police officers in its icy grip, slicing at them with razor-edged particles of snow.

Soon, George Bateson and Ed Riopel were completely lost in the howling white wilderness. Hopelessly, they trudged on behind their labouring dog teams, facing almost certain death from exposure when darkness fell. There was no shelter. Ice began to form on the men's eyelids, making it difficult to see.

Suddenly, the crack of a whip sounded above the roar of the blizzard. Out of the swirling murk a dim shape materialized: the figure of a huge man, dressed in snow-white furs and driving a team of white dogs. The Mounties shouted at the top of their voices, but the man seemed not to hear them. He raced past, then wheeled away into the driving snow. Desperately, the policemen plunged after him, realizing that this was perhaps their only hope of survival.

For two hours, Bateson and Riopel followed the mysterious stranger, pushing their dogs to the limit in an effort to keep up with him. At last, through a lull in the snowstorm, they saw an isolated outpost up ahead. A curtain of snow swept across their path again, and when it lifted the white-clad stranger had disappeared.

At the end of their strength, the policemen stumbled into the shelter of the outpost. Some trappers were already there. As they thawed out over a fire, Bateson and Riopel told the trappers what had happened. They wanted to know who their guide had been. They knew that they had to thank him for saving their lives. The trappers looked at each other in silence. At last, one of the older men took his pipe from his mouth and broke the hush.

"It was the Smoker who brought you in," he told them, "but you'll never be able to thank him for it this side of eternity. He's been dead for close on 30 years."

● RIGHT In 1978, one day after the death of his mother, Swiss metal-bender Silvio took a walk in the woods and saw a luminous ball. He photographed it, and the resulting picture revealed an angelic figure surrounded by a golden haze.

Saved by a phantom. An incredible story – but the weird stranger who brought Bateson and Riopel to safety on that day in 1949 was more than just a figment of the imagination. For more than a thousand men claim to have seen the Smoker, and his life-saving exploits are legendary throughout northeast Canada.

The Smoker was a real man. His name was Esau Dillingham, and for ten years – between 1910 and 1920 – he was one of the most notorious characters in Labrador. In that part of the world, the name "smoker" means someone who distils illegal liquor. For six years, Dillingham manufactured a potent brew from spruce cones, sugar and yeast, and peddled it up and down the territory. For Dillingham, the trade proved highly profitable – but a lot of people who drank his brew went blind or raving mad.

The law finally caught up with him in 1916. After drinking too much of Dillingham's "moonshine", some trappers got involved in a knife-fight and one of them was killed. The Smoker was sentenced to a year's imprisonment in St John's, Newfoundland.

Prison didn't cure Dillingham. He took up his illicit trade again almost as soon as he was released, but this time he was determined to escape the long arm of the Mounted Police. To camouflage his movements across the snow-covered countryside, he made himself a white suit of fox fur and ermine and acquired a team of 14 white dogs. He was chased by police several times, but each time he simply merged with the snowscape and vanished.

The Smoker's base – and his illegal still – were located in a wood near a place called Brazil's Pinch. He surrounded the spot with deadly, concealed bear traps that could turn a man's leg to pulp. He was arrested only once, in 1919. After two days of questions and threats, the police were forced to let him go through lack of evidence.

A few months later, he kidnapped a woman visiting the territory – and held her to ransom. The money he demanded didn't materialize, so he forced his unfortunate prisoner to drink his moonshine. When he released her she was out of her mind.

After that, the Smoker began to drink his own brew – and it proved to be his downfall. One day, while fighting drunk, he picked an argument with an Indian and broke the man's back with his bare hands. The police were really out to get the Smoker now – but when they did, it was too late to bring him to trial. In the winter of 1920, he broke his back in a fall and died in a police station on Frenchman's Island three days later. When he knew he that he was dying, Dillingham did something he had never done in his life before. He prayed. And these, according to witnesses, were his dying words: "Lord, I know I've been wicked, but I don't want to go to hell. Let me drive my team across this land until the end of time, so that I can undo the wrongs I've done."

They buried him the following day. It was the end of the Smoker and his evil. Or was it? One night two months later, a trapper reached the shelter of Frenchman's Island during a blinding snowstorm. He said that he would never have found the place at all, it he had not followed the figure of a "big man dressed all in white furs". But no one else arrived on the island that night.

Since then, hundreds of trappers in Labrador – hard-headed men, not given to superstition or wild imaginings – swear that the Smoker has appeared to lead them to safety when all seemed lost. Maybe his spectre still haunts the Labrador wastes, atoning for the sins he committed 75 years ago.

The legend of Captain Bayliss

● **ABOVE** In Flanders Fields . . . German soldiers surrendering during the battle of Neuve Chapelle, where Captain Terence Bayliss was killed.

In March 1915, while Esau Dillingham was at the peak of his nefarious activities in Labrador, the 39th Gharwal Rifle Regiment was distinguishing itself in the bloody battle of Neuve Chapelle, Flanders. These tough fighters, mostly hunters and herdsmen from the foothills of the Himalayas, formed part of the Indian Army Corps that had been sent to France in 1914.

At Neuve Chapelle, in a series of savage, almost suicidal attacks on the German trenches, the Indian troops covered themselves with battle honours. In one assault, the Rifles stormed into the enemy trenches under fierce shellfire and held them after bitter hand-to-hand fighting. They suffered many casualties that day, and one of them was the regimental adjutant, Captain Terence Bayliss.

The men of the regiment mourned him, for Bayliss's courage had done much to sustain the Indian troops in earlier fighting, as they became accustomed to the horrors of modern war. His body was never found. Officially, he was listed as "missing, presumed killed". Replacement troops arrived from India to take the place of those who had died, and in the space of just a few short months the regiment's former adjutant was remembered by only a handful of veterans.

Then, in September, 1915, something strange happened – something weird and mysterious that turned the memory of Captain Bayliss into a legend. It was during an attack just before the Battle of Loos: a company of Indian troops was pinned down on a hillside 50 yards (50 metres) from the enemy trenches by murderous machine gun and shell-fire, unable to withdraw or advance. Suddenly, a shadowy figure appeared on the fringe of a swirling cloud of dust and smoke – a British officer on a white horse, beckoning the men on towards the enemy.

In the superstitious minds of those soldiers who had been through the Neuve Chapelle battle, there was no doubt that it was Captain Bayliss. Shells were bursting all around the apparition, but it stood there unharmed, still waving the men on. The Indians were far more afraid of the supernatural than of anything the enemy could throw at them; with a roar, they charged through the withering fire and poured into the German trenches. After ten minutes of frantic bayonet-work, it was all over. They had captured their objective. As the smoke of the battle drifted away, the Indians fearfully scanned the shell-scarred ground for another glimpse of the man on the white horse. But the apparition had gone.

The spirit of Abraham Lincoln

There are many recorded cases of hauntings involving ghosts which appear to have a purpose in the afterlife: to watch benevolently over places and people. Not all of them, though, are as famous as President Abraham Lincoln, whose life was cut short by an assassin's bullet on 14 April 1865.

The reports of Lincoln's ghost being seen in the White House over the years are numerous. President Roosevelt never saw the spectre of his distinguished predecessor, but once confided to his biographer, Carl Sandburg, that when he had been alone in the Blue Room, overlooking the Washington Monument, he had felt a strong and comforting presence which he felt in some way was associated with Lincoln.

Roosevelt remained convinced that the spirit of Abraham Lincoln lived on in the White House. So too did Roosevelt's successor, Harry S. Truman, who later revealed that during his presidential term he was roused

● LEFT President Abraham Lincoln, whose benevolent ghost has been seen many times by tenants and visitors to the White House. Lincoln apparently had considerable psychic power, and had a visionary dream of his own assassination.

several times by a rapping on his bedroom door, but when he opened the door, there was nobody there.

Queen Wilhelmina of the Netherlands was also awakened by a knocking at her bedroom door when she was staying at the White House.

● FAR LEFT The coronation of Queen Wilhelmina of The Netherlands. While staying at the White House as a guest, she answered a night-time knock at the door of her room and saw the ghost of President Lincoln standing there. She promptly fainted.

● LEFT Queen Wilhelmina pictured later in life.

No one answered her permission to enter, so she got out of bed and went to open the door herself. A moment later, she had fallen to the floor in a faint. Later she confessed to a very concerned President Roosevelt that she had seen the figure of the late President Lincoln standing there.

Lincoln's appearances have sometimes been accompanied by the sound of his loud, booming laugh, one of his characteristics. At other times, his ghost has displayed different moods. He has been seen walking slowly and sadly through the East Room, where his body lay in state, and standing at the window of the Oval Room, gazing out towards Virginia, seemingly lost in thought. On another occasion a maid, Mary Eban, burst into Mrs Roosevelt's study in a state of great agitation and reported that she had just seen the ghost in the Lincoln Room. The spectral figure of the dead president had been seen sitting on the edge of the bed, taking his boots off.

Many more tenants of the White House have seen Abraham Lincoln's ghost. One theory behind the fairly frequent appearances

is that he expended so much energy in fulfilling his duties during the terrible years of the Civil War, that part of it lingers on, integrated into the fabric of the White House itself, and manifests itself in his form from time to time. On top of this, President Lincoln himself apparently had psychic power; the

fact that he had a visionary dream of his own assassination is history, and it is also known that he held seances in the White House.

While Abraham Lincoln's ghost wanders the rooms of the place into which he poured so much of his spirit, another friendly ghost belongs firmly in the great outdoors.

● ABOVE The White House. One theory behind Lincoln's frequent appearances is that he expended so much energy during the terrible years of the Civil War that some of it became part of the building.

● BELOW Originally known as the Guardsman, the Grenadier Inn in Old Barrack Yard, Wilton Row, London, is reputed to be haunted in the month of September by an officer who was flogged to death after being caught cheating at cards.

After the Loos battle, the Gharwal Rifles – together with other units of the Indian Corps – were sent to the Suez Canal area, and after a year of duty there they returned to India to be reorganized before going back on active service.

One night in 1917, the orderly officer set out to make his usual inspection of the guard. The officers' mess was in a villa about a mile away from the main barracks, which was reached by way of a narrow road through the forest. Together with his orderly NCO, the officer climbed the hill that overlooked the parade ground, expecting the customary challenge from the sentry on duty at the top. He would then give the password, and the guard would turn out for inspection. But no challenge came – and a minute later, the officer saw that the men on guard duty were already lined up in two neat ranks. Moreover, they were looking around fearfully and whispering among themselves. The sergeant of the guard was peering over a stone wall that ran along the side of the hill; beyond it, there was a sheer drop of 20 to 30 feet (6–9 m).

The orderly officer listened in disbelief as the sergeant told his story. The man was obviously frightened, which was uncharacteristic of him; the medals on his chest testified to his courage.

A few minutes before the orderly officer arrived, he said, he had heard the sentry challenge someone. The sergeant had called out into the darkness, wanting to know who it was – and the sentry had replied "Orderly Officer's rounds". The sergeant had immediately ordered the guard to turn out for inspection, and a moment later he had seen an officer on a white horse standing as motionless as a statue in front of the sentry. The officer had returned the sergeant's salute – and without saying a word or making any attempt to dismount, he had ridden around the guard, looking critically at the soldiers' turnout. Then before the eyes of the astonished men, the mysterious officer had wheeled his horse and leaped over the stone wall.

Together with the sergeant and the orderly NCO, the orderly officer searched the ground below the wall. They found nothing, not even a hoofprint.

A week later, the mysterious officer appeared again. Once more, he inspected the guard thoroughly – and this time he spoke. In a voice that the men described as "faint and hollow", he ordered the guard NCO to report one of the riflemen for having a tunic button undone. Then, as before, he took a flying leap over the stone wall and vanished – but not before the veteran NCO had positively identified him as the late Captain Bayliss.

Like wildfire, the word spread around the barracks that Bayliss's spirit had come back to keep an eye on the smartness of the soldiers. The officers of the Regiment began to grow worried in case the apparitiion had an effect on the moral of the men. It did – but not in the way the officers had expected. Before the visits of the former adjutant, the soldiers had been immaculate; now they sparkled.

After a few months, there was hardly a man in the whole regiment who had not seen the spectre of Captain Bayliss. His ghostly guard inspections ceased when the 39th Gharwal Rifles were sent on active service to Mesopotamia in 1918, but resumed as soon as the Regiment returned to India after the war.

For two years, the visitations of Captain Bayliss were regular occurrences. Then, one night in 1920, a nervous young sentry loosed off a round of ammunition at the phantom, which abruptly vanished.

The sentry was reprimanded for the "unwarranted expenditure of one round of government ammunition at a ghost". The ghost of Captain Terence Bayliss was never seen again.

Or was it?

After World War II, when India became independent, the Royal Gharwal Rifles ceased to be part of the British Army. Late in 1947, in a moving ceremony at the old barracks beneath the towering Himalayas, the Regiment bade farewell to the British officers who had led it to even more battle honours in the bitter war against the Japanese. As the sun touched the horizon, the haunting notes of the Last Post echoed across the parade ground and the Union Flag was lowered for the last time.

It may have been a trick of the light, or just the tears in the eyes of many a hardened soldier. But there were those who swore afterwards that a figure appeared briefly on the hilltop overlooking the barracks; the figure of a man in the uniform of 30 years ago, his arm raised in rigid salute as the flag came fluttering down. A man on a white horse.

● BELOW The Blue Lion Inn at Cwm, North Wales, is haunted by the ghost of a farm labourer. He is quite a familiar sight, and a considerable tourist attraction.

One old farmhouse in Hampshire, England, is haunted by the ghost of the lady with the beautiful smile. There has been a dwelling of some sort on the site since Anglo-Saxon times; the present building was bought in a derelict state just after World War II and renovated. The ghost began to appear in 1969 and has been seen at intervals over the years. She is a young, slim woman, wrapped in a cloak with an attached hood, and her face stands out with great clarity. It seems to radiate a distinct feeling of peace and tranquillity.

Is she, too, keeping a supernatural watch over a place she once loved?

● **ABOVE** Burgh Castle, Norfolk, England, is actually an old Roman fortress. Phantom legionaries may still be seen there, standing on the ramparts and gazing watchfully out over the North Sea in defence of Britain's shores.

Theatrical ghosts

The ghosts of Esau Dillingham and Terence Bayliss each had a friendly purpose: to succour those in desperate need in Dillingham's case, and to maintain the pride of a beloved regiment in Bayliss's. Tales of benevolent ghosts in the theatre are not uncommon: a spirit known as Jake – the ghost of a stagehand who was accidentally killed in 1942 – is said to haunt His Majesty's Theatre in Aberdeen; he generally keeps a spectral eye on things, has been known to move items of equipment from one place to another, and acts as a kind of guardian angel when someone gets into trouble. On one occasion, a scenic artist was spraying some gold paint on scenery when he accidentally sprayed some into his eyes. Blinded, and in great pain, he was frantically wondering how he was going to get to the washroom when, suddenly, "something" else took charge. The man was guided to the washroom by unseen hands, and within seconds he was dabbing the paint from his eyes.

Eastern Airlines Flight 401

Friendly ghosts of a different kind appear to be the spectral legacy of a terrible air crash. On the night of Friday, 29 December 1972, Eastern Airlines Flight 401 from New York to Miami crashed in the Florida Everglades during its approach to land at Miami airport. The aircraft, a Lockheed TriStar, was completely destroyed. Seventy people survived the accident, which was apparently caused by a combination of pilot error and equipment failure, but 110 passengers and crew were killed.

Not long after the Flight 401 disaster, rumours began to circulate among employees of Eastern Airlines that the ghosts of Captain Bob Loft and flight engineer Don Repo, both of whom were killed in the crash, had been seen on other Eastern flights. Most of the sightings occurred – or allegedly occurred – on board a TriStar that was the lost aircraft's "sister ship", the two having been purchased at the same time by Eastern. It was also said, but never confirmed, that parts of the crashed TriStar had been used as spares in the other aircraft.

American writer John G. Fuller, who specialized in unexplained phenomena such as UFOs, heard the rumours and carried out his own investigation into them. The result was a very readable book, *The Ghost of Flight 401*, which was published in 1976. In it, Fuller claimed that the ghost of Dan Repo, looking very solid and wearing the uniform of an Eastern Airlines Second Officer, had been seen by the flight engineer of the sister TriStar. Repo allegedly told him not to worry about the preflight (the check that ensures all engineering systems are functioning properly) because he had already done it. The ghost then vanished.

Captain Loft, it was said, was also seen in the first class section of a TriStar at New York's John F. Kennedy Airport by the aircraft captain and two flight attendants. Loft spoke to them before he disappeared. The flight was cancelled.

If these stories and others like them are true, it seems that Loft and Repo appeared to their former colleagues in spirit form because they were anxious to prevent others experiencing the kind of disaster that had overwhelmed them.

The story is by no means unique. There are others like it, dotted through the annals of aviation. Who can say what the last thoughts of a pilot might be, when he knows beyond all doubt that he and his passengers and crew are seconds away from violent death?

We know, however, what the last words of lost pilots often are, because they feature time and again on the tapes recovered from the flight recorders of crashed aircraft.

"I'm sorry . . ."

● **ABOVE** The title page of the Evening News, reporting on the crash of the Eastern Airlines flight 401. The ghosts of the captain and the flight engineer have appeared to other airmen.

What Are Ghosts?

arlier in this book, some attempt was made to explain the poltergeist phenomenon by laying the blame on the forces unleashed, either deliberately or inadvertently, by the human psyche.

Apparitions present a different problem. Ghosts can be seen, although their aspect assumes varying degrees of "firmness"; sometimes they are ephemeral, indistinct shapes, bearing only a hazy resemblance to a physical form, but often they appear solid enough to touch. Indeed, on many occasions people have reached out to touch what they assumed must be a real person, only to have their hands pass through the spectre, see it suddenly disappear or pass through a solid wall. Such apparitions have even been photographed, although this happens infrequently.

● BELOW A white-draped figure, double exposed against a suitable background, can be made to appear as a traditional ghost.

Researchers into the paranormal have found it much easier to record the noises made by ghosts: cries, voices, footsteps, doors opening and closing and so on. Phantom smells are also often reported in connection with a haunting; these are usually pleasant aromas such as tobacco smoke, perfume or even food being cooked. It has often proved possible, too, to established the presence of a ghost by touch, when the ghost itself cannot be seen. During the peak Christmas shopping period in Cambridgeshire, England, some years ago, assistants in a high street shoe shop claimed to have heard strange noises – footsteps on the stairs and in the rooms above the shop. When the floor of an unused upstairs room was sprinkled with talcum powder, small footprints were discovered when the room was opened the next morning. There are many similar instances.

One noticeable, and physically measurable, aspect of most hauntings is a sudden drop in temperature, a very interesting phenomenon. The temperature of a body is a measure of its "hotness", which can be defined as a property determining the rate at which heat is transferred to or from it.

Temperature is therefore a measure of the kinetic energy of the molecules, atoms or ions of which matter is composed. However, under certain conditions a space may be created in which there are no molecules or atoms: such a space is called a vacuum. A perfect vacuum is unobtainable, since every material which surrounds a space has a definite vapour pressure, so the term is generally taken to mean a space containing air or gas at very low pressure. As pressure decreases, so does temperature. So, when an apparition manifests itself, it creates a partial vacuum, with a resulting drop in pressure and temperature. How the ghost does this is, as yet, an intriguing scientific mystery.

So is the question of how, and why, ghosts appear in the first place. Apart from cases involving hoaxes, frauds, an excess of alcohol or simply an over-active imagination, there are several rational explanations. The first is that people who claim to have seen a ghost have been the victims of hallucination.

This theory implies that people draw subconsciously on stored images in their minds and project them as phantoms. It might be plausible enough if a person is in a semi-conscious state, emerging

for example, as radio waves, infra-red rays, ultra-violet rays, light, X-rays and gamma rays. All of these radiations are emitted by matter in the form of photons.

The imprint theory suggests that an electromagnetic field may be influenced by deep human emotions such as anger, sadness, fear or extreme happiness, emotions that are characteristic of most hauntings. An event such as a violent murder can release radiations that imprint themselves on the electromagnetic environment. The imprint is indestructible, and under certain favourable conditions it may be released in a visible form. This action may be triggered by emissions from an "aware" human mind, which might account for the fact that psychics and mediums experience ghostly phenomena more frequently than unattuned people.

● LEFT This spectral image of a woman on a staircase provides a good example of how simple it is to fake a "ghost" photograph.

● BELOW Another faked photograph depicts a magician with a sword.

from sleep for example, but it has a lot of flaws. It does not explain sightings by several witnesses, nor does it explain noises and smells.

The so-called "imprint theory" is more plausible, and depends on an understanding of electromagnetism. Electric and magnetic phenomena are fundamental to the laws of physics. The two interact to create an electromagnetic field, in which the principal particle is the photon. The electromagnetic field produces radiation – waves of energy – of varying frequencies which manifest themselves,

● ABOVE A "ghost" photograph taken inside Newby Church, Yorkshire, England, in the early 1960s. The spectre, unseen at the time, showed up when the film was developed. The man behind the camera was the Reverend K.F. Lord.

But this theory also has its flaws. It does not account for ghostly noises, nor does it account for physical phenomena such as the movement of solid objects or the opening and shutting of doors. Moreover, if an electromagnetic imprint of a traumatic occasion can be unlocked, by whatever process, it is logical to assume that the resulting image would depict the event itself. In all but a few cases, it does not. What manifests itself is the "lost soul" of the person involved.

Another intriguing theory is that ghosts are the manifestations of people living a "life between life" – in other words, trapped in a kind of limbo between successive incarnations. Investigators into the phenomenon of reincarnation claim to have interviewed subjects who have memories of visiting strange places in their between-life phases. Ghosts, in other words, can be considered the shades of people weaving in and out of incarnations on some

long odyssey. The theory might seem far-fetched, but no more so than one that suggests that ghosts are really physical people belonging to a parallel universe – people who somehow cross over into our own area of space and time for brief periods. The theory is a complex one, involving as it does a study of the nature of time itself. One idea compares the passage of time to a deck of cards shuffled at random; the shuffling destroys the order of things and produces a jumble. A higher card in the sequence, although it is still distinguishable as just that, suddenly appears lower in the pack. So is time subject to random shuffles of some kind, and if so do people – and objects – appear out of phase until the pack, so to speak, is reshuffled? If so, and if time is a two-way journey, why do ghosts always appear in the garb of time past, and never of the future? This is the major flaw in that argument.

If all these theories fail to hold water, we are left with just one – that ghosts really are apparitions from some world that exists beyond death. Setting aside religious aspects, with their concepts of heaven, hell and purgatory, we must try to seek a scientific explanation.

The scientific and accepted fact is that nothing really dies; it merely changes into something else. A human body may seem to be destroyed, but in fact its component atoms become part of the environment under the action of earth, fire or water, while the electomagnetic force known as the soul goes somewhere else – into another realm, dimension, call it what you will.

Is it stretching the imagination too much to believe that a life force, or soul, that has become part of what we could term the cosmic consciousness might, under certain circumstances, intrude into our physical, material realm to produce what we call a haunting? The answer to this is no, and if we can accept that, we can move on to another very important point.

Somewhere along the line, ghostly manifestations are inextricably linked with the power of the human psyche, and science is only just beginning to unlock that power. When it succeeds – and that day may not be too distant – we shall have the answers to questions that have intrigued humanity for centuries. And the mysteries of the spirit world may be mysteries no longer.

● ABOVE The main square of Kronborg Castle, Elsinore, Denmark, where traitors were executed in medieval times. The sound of the axe delivering its fearsome death blow can still be heard on occasion.

● OPPOSITE Culloden House, Inverness, is reported to be haunted by the ghost of the unhappy "Bonny Prince Charlie", whose aspirations to be king of England and Scotland were destroyed on Culloden battlefield by disciplined troops on 16 April 1746.

Index

Picture Credits